THE HOODS

THE HOODS

Crime and Punishment in Belfast

Heather Hamill

PRINCETON UNIVERSITY PRESS

PRINCETON & OXFORD

Copyright © 2011 by Princeton University Press

Published by Princeton University Press, 41 William Street, Princeton,
New Jersey 08540

In the United Kingdom: Princeton University Press, 6 Oxford Street,
Woodstock, Oxfordshire OX20 1TW

press.princeton.edu

All Rights Reserved

Library of Congress Cataloging-in-Publication Data
Hamill, Heather, 1971–
The hoods : crime and punishment in Belfast / Heather Hamill.
    p.   cm.

Includes bibliographical references and index.

ISBN 978-0-691-11963-2 (cloth : alk. paper) 1. Crime—Northern
Ireland—Belfast. 2. Criminals—Northern Ireland—Belfast. 3. Juvenile
delinquents—Northern Ireland—Belfast. 4. Punishment—Northern
Ireland—Belfast. 5. Paramilitary forces—Northern Ireland—Belfast.
I. Title.

HV6949.N67H36 2011
364.9416'7—dc22   2010014342

British Library Cataloging-in-Publication Data is available

This book has been composed in Giovanni Std and Din Pro

Printed on acid-free paper ∞

Printed in the United States of America

10 9 8 7 6 5 4 3 2 1

For my parents

CONTENTS

ACKNOWLEDGMENTS

This research began as the basis for my doctoral thesis in the Department of Sociology at the University of Oxford under the supervision of Diego Gambetta, whose influence is writ large across this book. I am indebted to him for his patient intellectual guidance and critical eye. He gave me the confidence and support I needed to keep going, and this book would never have been completed without him. Stephanie Allen, Edmund Chattoe-Brown, Paddy Hillyard, Roger Hood, Valeria Pizzini-Gambetta, and Federico Varese all contributed very useful comments on earlier drafts of this work. My thanks also go to Ian Malcolm at Princeton University Press for his patience and support and to Linda Truilo for her excellent copyediting. I am also extremely grateful to the British Academy for granting me a postdoctoral fellowship that enabled me to carry out additional fieldwork needed for this book.

The primary obstacle in carrying out this research was gaining access to the groups and individuals who are the subjects of the research. Colin Roberts's very practical support at the beginning of this work was invaluable in helping me to negotiate access to a variety of field resources that made this research possible The Probation Board for Northern Ireland eased my path considerably. In particular, Breidge Gadd and Brian Mc-Caughey facilitated access to a number of statutory and voluntary agencies and introduced me to the West Belfast Youth at Risk Programme.

I owe an immense debt to the staff and volunteers of West Belfast Youth at Risk, who allowed me squatter's rights in their office and helped me gain access to many of the young people who participated in this research. My special thanks go to Jimmy Quinn and Angela Morris, and I am especially indebted to Mark Jordan for his insights into life on the "wild side."

On a more personal note, fieldwork can be a lonely endeavor, and I am sincerely grateful to Julie Wilson and Arthur Magill for their friendship during this time. My husband, Steve Fisher, inherited this project with me and has helped me in every possible way—thank you for everything.

If I have gone any way to understanding crime and punishment in Belfast, it is primarily because people were willing to talk to me about the issues affecting their lives. Therefore, I thank each individual who participated in this research and in particular the young people who talked to me. In the main, they responded with openness, honesty, intelligence, and humor. I am deeply saddened that three of these young people have recently died under very tragic circumstances.

On January 16, 1999, the headline in the *Andersonstown News,* West Belfast's local newspaper, read "Joyriding: The scourge returns." The paper reported that the evening before, forty-two stolen cars were abandoned in West Belfast, "many of them burned out, while others were seriously damaged or vandalised."[1] There followed a series of articles over the following months detailing the damage caused by young people driving stolen cars recklessly and often under the influence of alcohol and drugs. This included the tragic death of Patrick Hanna, who was killed when a stolen car traveling at approximately 100 mph jumped the pavement in a residential area and struck him. An eyewitness described what happened afterward: "Other joyriders returned shortly after the ambulance and police left and started doing hand-brake turns at the police tape where the man had been killed. I couldn't believe that anyone could be that cruel and heartless."[2] This incident followed a similar accident in which seven-year-old Eamon Armstrong was killed when he, too, was struck by a stolen car. His mother and her partner were seriously injured: "With two deaths and so many injuries in the space of such a short time, there's a real sense that the joyriders have taken over the streets and that anyone could be the next victim,"[3] reported the *Andersonstown News.* When joyriders smashed a stolen car into a school bus carrying pupils to school during rush hour traffic, the culprits were condemned as "worse than irresponsible."[4] In March 2000, District Nurse Maureen Sheehan was killed when a car driven by a joyrider caused a three-car collision on the Falls Road. In the same week, John McDonald, another local resident, was killed in a hit-and-run accident.[5]

For West Belfast residents, a disrupted night's sleep is all too common. Night raids by the British army and the police were a familiar feature throughout the 1970s, 1980s, and early 1990s. The noise of rioting and shots being fired in gun battles between Republican paramilitaries and the security forces, or between Republican and Loyalist paramilitaries, once kept many households awake. In recent years, however, it has been the screech of tires and the roar of car engines that has terrorized local residents:

> You go to bed at night and then you'd hear the car screechin' somewhere outside. Then, you get frightened about your property and car outside in case they ram into it. You're lying there wonderin' where they are, and if they'll come down your street. Then you jump up out of bed, and there's even more fear about the car, and who's in it, and what if they crash and hurt themselves or hurt someone else who you know. And then you start calling them "wee bastards" because they keep you awake at night. Part of you wishes they'd just crash and get it over with, and let you go back to sleep. (Local Resident H)

Young people (mostly males) steal cars from areas throughout Greater Belfast and beyond and drive them to their home neighborhoods in West Belfast. There are rough estimates of between 50 and 100 different cars being raced recklessly around West Belfast's residential areas on any given night. Several of the area's estates, or housing developments, such as Poleglass and Turf Lodge, are encircled by ring roads, which provide ideal racing circuits for joyriders who describe a sort of relay race where they steal a car in one area, race it to another area, abandon it, and steal another car, and so on until they end up at the finish, somewhere in West Belfast. Most joyriding tends to take place at night, but an audacious few will joyride during the day: "There was a car going fuckin' nuts during the day. It looked like an 18-year-old drivin' with a 14-year-old wee lad in beside him. The neighbours were going nuts and screamin' 'fuckin' bastards' at them. Her up the road was standin' at the corner waitin' for them to come back round again, so she could throw somethin' at them" (Local Resident H). An entourage often accompanies the joyriders; in some instances up to 100 young people will gather to watch them race their cars around.[6]

Joyriding is not unique to Belfast; the English cities of Newcastle upon Tyne and Oxford have experienced sporadic episodes of it. Nor is it simply a contemporary phenomenon: The term "joyride" arrived in the United Kingdom from the United States in 1912 and was defined as "a ride at high speed, esp. in a motor car."[7] The theft of motor vehicles for temporary use was first legislated against in the United Kingdom in

1930.[8] Belfast's struggle in dealing with this problem, however, is unique and worthy of investigation, given the number of incidents its residents report; the joyriders' imperviousness to the many diversionary initiatives that the city's statutory criminal justice agencies have implemented and that have been successful elsewhere; and the particular risks of incurring violent retribution from paramilitaries. According to police statistics, on average, 480 individuals are convicted of car theft each year in Northern Ireland, the vast majority for the offense of Taking and Driving Away (hereafter TDA), which is the closest official appropriation to joyriding. For example, in 1995 there were a total of 542 car theft convictions: 530 for TDA and only 12 for the offense of car theft.[9] In addition, 88 percent of those convicted of TDA and released from prison in the period January 1995 to the end of November 1996 were Catholic, and almost all came from West Belfast.[10] Protestant young people do not seem to joyride to the same extent, a point that will be returned to in later chapters.

Where there is crime, there is also punishment, and a major by-product of the political and civil conflict in Northern Ireland has been a lack of consensus among the population over who should police ordinary crime and how. This is clearly evidenced among the predominantly Nationalist and Republican inhabitants of West Belfast, who have consistently sought to prevent crime and punish offenders by employing a variety of informal strategies, rather than rely upon the police service. The most notorious of these informal approaches are shootings, beatings, and exclusions by Republican armed groups. The police began recording casualties of shootings in 1973 and beatings in 1988. Between 1973 and March 2007, 2463 nonmilitary shootings and assaults had been attributed to Republican paramilitary groups.[11] These figures are the tip of the iceberg, and many victims who receive less serious injuries or who have been threatened, placed on a curfew, or exiled from their homes never report the incident. The police do not record which organization is responsible for each incident, but the Irish Republican Army (hereafter IRA) is the largest and most powerful Republican armed group, and it is thought to be responsible for most attacks.

Protestant Loyalist armed groups also shoot, beat, exile, curfew, and warn members of their own community. The Ulster Volunteer Force (hereafter UVF) and the Ulster Defence Association (hereafter UDA) are the two largest armed Protestant groups and carry out most of these attacks. According to police statistics, between 1973 and March 2007 they shot and assaulted 2558 people.[12]

The paramilitary groups use these informal methods against members of their own communities only. These attacks are not sectarian and are commonly used by armed groups to "punish" young petty offenders, known locally as "hoods," or those who have defected from, disobeyed, or crossed an armed group in some way.

The use of the term "punishment" to describe these attacks has been contested. The Independent Monitoring Commission (hereafter IMC), established in 2004 to report on the activities of paramilitary groups to the British and Irish governments, stated that the term "punishment beating" is misleading and "lends spurious respectability to these attacks and underplays their violence."[13] However, people in communities most affected by this violence use the term "punishment" to describe these attacks, and so throughout this book I will use the term "paramilitary punishment attack" (hereafter PPA) to describe a nonmilitary shooting or beating of a civilian by a Republican or Loyalist paramilitary group.

This violence has taken place within the broader context of the political violence in Northern Ireland in which, as of 1998, "thirty years after the conflict started[,] one in seven of the population reported having been a victim of violence; one in seven had a family member killed or injured; and one in four had been caught up in an explosion."[14] As figure 1 illustrates, however, PPAs perpetrated by paramilitary organizations against members of their own religious communities follow a rhythm different from that of deaths perpetrated by the paramilitary organizations and resulting from the political conflict.

Deaths attributed to paramilitaries peaked in 1977, and the trend has been downward since then. On the other hand, the number of PPAs increased dramatically in the 1990s, peaking in 1997 and again in 2002. Explanations for these trends will be discussed throughout this book.

Local informal responses to crime have been in operation in many areas in Northern Ireland, but the number of initiatives and the frequency of more violent approaches have been the greatest in Catholic West Bel-

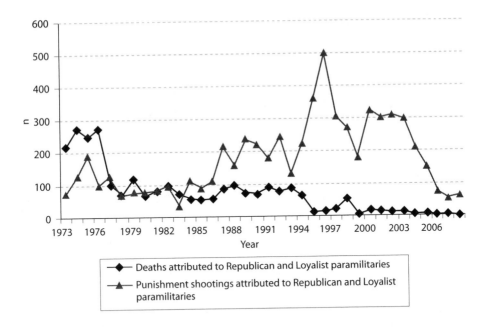

Figure 1 Deaths and punishment shootings and assaults attributed to Republican and Loyalist groups 1973–2008. *Source*: Author's compilation from Sutton 2010; PSNI 2003, 2009. Punishment beatings were recorded officially from 1982 onward.

fast, and consequently this area was chosen as the primary research setting. The initial aim of this research was to carry out a systematic study of the structure and process of informal community punishment in West Belfast, and to examine the interface between the informal community system and the statutory criminal justice system. Two primary research questions were formulated:

1. Why do residents in West Belfast choose to report crime to the IRA and support the often brutal system of informal justice?
2. Why do Sinn Féin and the IRA continue to be involved in policing and punishing offenders in West Belfast despite the negative political consequences of these actions?

While these questions remained central to the research, after embarking on fieldwork I realized that it was going to be possible to access the young people who are most at risk of becoming victims of PPAs, and so two further questions became part of this research:

3. Why do the hoods act in the way they do, for no apparent material reward? Are their actions purely the expression of irrationality?

4. Furthermore, why do harsh physical paramilitary punishments not have a *specific deterrent* effect on a small minority of offenders in West Belfast but rather seem to encourage them?

These four questions guided the data collection for the study and the structure of this book.

Method and Data

RESEARCH STRATEGY

Given the sensitive nature of the research topics and the difficulties of accessing hidden or reticent populations, I felt that qualitative methods would provide the most appropriate research approach. Various authors have argued that topics of a sensitive kind remain unsuited to study by means of large impersonal studies.[15] Indeed, toward the end of the field-work period an article appeared in the *Andersonstown News,* a local West Belfast newspaper, warning residents not to respond to a questionnaire from the University of Luton containing questions relating to residents' religious beliefs and support for the Republican Movement. The article noted that these were "not the sort of queries you'd be inclined to post to a stranger in England."[16] I decided that the research questions could best be explored by conducting an ethnographic study in West Belfast. In line with ethnographic tradition, this study involved extended time engaged in fieldwork; the generation of descriptive and multiple sources of data; the development of close relationships with respondents; and detailed understandings of the research site.[17]

RESEARCH GROUPS

Three primary research groups were targeted and interviewed using semis-tructured and unstructured interview techniques throughout an eighteen-month fieldwork period between 1997 and 1999. The first group was a cross-section of residents in West Belfast. Unstructured discussions and semistructured interviews were carried out with fifty respondents who all lived or worked in West Belfast. The first respondents were a snowball sample generated from two local community groups where I became a volunteer and from contacts given to me by the Probation Board for Northern Ireland. In an attempt to bring more variation into this sample, I selected respondents on the basis of their knowledge and experience of living in West Belfast and their expressed views on the informal system of policing and punishment. The sample included those who supported the system, those who actively opposed it, and others who were relatively indifferent to it. Many of the respondents were active in local initiatives, such as community and youth projects, and to some degree these individuals can be seen as opinion formers within West Belfast.

The second research group comprised members of Sinn Féin and the IRA. Generally in West Belfast, PPAs are discussed among residents in hushed tones. When someone is punished, local people often refer to the attack as "being done," and are unwilling to discuss the issues or the processes in any detail. Furthermore, membership in the IRA is illegal, and physically assaulting or shooting people are criminal offenses. Those individuals in West Belfast who have been involved in perpetrating these sorts of paramilitary activities are reluctant to identify themselves and to talk in-depth about their experiences. I was able to overcome the combined problems of restricted access to informed respondents, issue sensitivity, and informant reticence in a number of ways during the fieldwork period. The ten respondents who were members of the IRA were accessed not as members of the IRA but via their other roles within West Belfast as youth and community workers, taxi drivers, parents and grandparents. The issues were discussed either as a specific topic of an interview or as a point of interest that came about during impromptu conversations and discussions. These conversations where often the most informative and arose gradually after I had spent a lengthy period of time in the community building up trust and associating with informants' friends and acquaintances. Among these informants were a former senior figure in the IRA's policing activities and those who had carried out PPAs. All of these respondents had served prison sentences for their involvement in the IRA and are identified in the book as "ex-prisoners." Other data were gathered from discussions with politically nonaligned residents in West Belfast.

The third research group was made up of seventy-two young people involved in criminal and antisocial behavior and known locally as hoods. Contact with the hoods was made with the help of the Probation Board for Northern Ireland and the West Belfast Youth at Risk Project. Each young person was interviewed at least once and ten ex-hoods were also interviewed at length. The identities of all respondents remain anonymous, and the names assigned to individual hoods are fictitious.

Interviews were also conducted with members of the Police Service of Northern Ireland (hereafter PSNI), which was formally the Royal Ulster Constabulary (RUC); the Probation Board for Northern Ireland (hereafter PBNI); the Northern Ireland Association for the Care and Resettlement of Offenders (hereafter NIACRO); the Simon Community; and Community Restorative Justice Ireland (hereafter CRJI).

Additional follow-up interviews were carried on in 2002 with members of each of the three research groups, including young people who grew up in the same circumstances as the hoods but did not get involved in crime and antisocial behavior. Further interviews were conducted between 2002 and 2005 with members of the UVF and the UDA.

DATA COLLECTION

Four different types of data were collected pertaining to the four research questions and the three research groups: academic literature, interview data, observational data, and data drawn from the analysis of documents, primarily articles from newspapers published in Northern Ireland: the *Andersonstown News, Irish News, Belfast Telegraph, Newsletter* and the *Irish Times*. Other documents analyzed included police and government reports dating from 1995 to 2006. In addition to the range of data collected and in order to combine the elements of what is considered to be "good" ethnography, a number of qualitative research methods were employed.[18] During participant observation in West Belfast, primary data were collected during interviews. While fifty semistructured interviews were carried out with local residents, the bulk of the interview data were collected during unstructured interviews. Hundreds of spontaneous, informal conversations took place ranging from short chats on a street corner at night with two or three hoods to more lengthy and involved discussions over cups of tea, cartons of chips, pints of beer, and cigarettes. Giving or receiving a lift in a car from a respondent would often result in a lengthy discussion. During these interviews and conversations I constantly kept the research questions in mind, sometimes initiating the topics of discussion, but more often allowing the conversation to flow naturally as issues specific to the research were raised and dropped a number of times in the course of a discussion.[19] From the outset of the fieldwork it became apparent that it was a mistake to ask respondents too many questions. Local people gave monosyllabic "yes" or "no" answers to direct questions about the research topics or evasively denied knowledge with comments such as "I keep out of all of that, you'd need to ask somebody else." In cases with all three research groups, direct questions were perceived as threatening and the answers provided were of little value. This resistance to direct questioning, particularly with members of the IRA and the hoods, proved to be very similar to Michael Agar's account of doing street research on drug addiction:

> In the streets, though I learned that you don't ask questions. There are at least two reasons for that rule. One is because a person is vulnerable to arrest by the police, or to being cheated or robbed by other street people. Questions about behavior may be asked to find out when you are vulnerable to arrest. Or they may be asked to find out when or in what way you can be parted from some money or heroin. Even if one sees no direct connection between the question and those outcomes, it might just be because one has not figured out the questioner's "game" yet.
>
> The second reason for not asking questions is that you should not have to ask. To be accepted in the streets is to be hip; to be hip is to be knowledgeable; to be knowledgeable is to be capable of understanding what is going on on the basis of minimal cues. So to ask a question is to show that you are not acceptable and this creates problems in a relationship when you have just been introduced to somebody.[20]

The lack of formality and explicitness of the interviews and conversations from which much of the data for this book has been gathered does raise the issue of the subject's consent. Obtaining consent in this context can be seen as the outcome of a developmental process.[21] The disclosure of sensitive, confidential, or controversial information or opinions is only possible in "these situations once trust has been established between the fieldworker and the people being studied. Where this has been done consent becomes implicit."[22] Thus in this study, five months of participant observation and general hanging around passed before interview data of any depth or richness was gathered.

The research topics, the characteristics of the respondents, and the unplanned nature of many of the interviews meant that I was often faced with the problem of discussing violent and criminal behavior. I was given details of crimes that had been committed, and also became privy to knowledge of crimes about to be perpetrated. In these instances I followed Federico Varese, who had taken guidance during his fieldwork on the Russian mafia from the advice given to priests and confessors in the sixteenth-century manuals created by the Roman Catholic Church at the time when a new doctrine of sin began to emerge in the Western Church: "Do not show amazement; or a contorted face; do not show revulsion (no matter what enormities are confessed); do not rebuke the penitent; or exclaim 'Oh, what vile sins!'"[23]

In the social sciences, the method of recording data affects the data itself.[24] Field notes were used for recording observational data. I constantly carried a notebook in which to jot down observations and on occasion used a voice recorder. There are a number of ways in which to record answers to questions during an unstructured interview: filming, tape-recording, note-taking, or memorizing and writing up afterward. Martyn Hammersley and Paul Atkinson consider tape-recording, supplemented by jotting notes on the nonverbal aspects and features of the physical setting, to provide the most "complete, concrete and detailed" data.[25] However, because of the ongoing political unrest and covert activities in West Belfast, residents have endured almost forty years of surveillance from the British security forces and are very wary of being recorded.

I was also acutely aware of my Northern Irish Protestant background and the fact that I was coming from an "establishment" English university (a fact that I did not advertise), and I did not want to be mistaken as a member of the British security forces. I did not want to be "caught" with an unexplained tape-recorder. I was concerned that, at best, the presence of a tape-recorder would label me from the outset as someone to be wary of, and hamper access to the research groups. I also suspected that taping interviews would inhibit the building up of trust between the interviewees and myself, and dissuade frankness. Many of the interviews were ad hoc, and I did not want to stop a free-flowing conversation in order to get a tape-recorder out of my bag. In addition, the topics discussed were often sensitive and involved details of criminal activities (tapes can be used in evidence in a manner that notes cannot). Varese records how at the beginning of his fieldwork he used a tape-recorder during interviews but found that it made his interview subjects feel very uncomfortable and they gave vague and evasive answers: "One interviewee, in particular was extremely vague and, at the end of the interview, he invited me to his house to have a 'proper' conversation."[26] From the outset, therefore, I decided not to tape-record interviews but to take notes whenever possible and rely upon memory at other times, writing up an account of the interview as soon as possible after the event. While this method is arguably the least reliable—as memory may easily fail, be selective, and leave out details—I judged that it was the only method that facilitated trust and flexibility in this particular research setting, and I made every attempt to record the essence of what was said.

The data collection method clearly raises questions of the validity and reliability of the findings.[27] As Hammersley suggests, "An account is valid or true if it represents accurately those features of the phenomena that it is intended to describe, explain or theorise. Assumed here, then, is a correspondence theory of truth, but the correspondence involves selective representation rather than reproduction of reality."[28] Given that it is impossible to know for certain whether an account is true, or the extent to which it is accurate, the validity of claims must be judged on the basis of the evidence offered in support of them.[29] For this book the task was to recognize the limits to establishing validity but, nevertheless, to strive toward it.[30] The ethnography, therefore, involved a combination of research procedures and data sources, and the technique of triangulation was used to assess the validity of inferences by examining data relating to the same concept from participant observation, interviewing, and documents.[31] Thus, in writing this account of crime and justice in West Belfast, I have attempted to weave the different forms of data together to tell a story that is both descriptive and analytical.

Theoretical Framework and Chapter Outline

This book examines extralegal policing and punishment in Belfast from the perspective of those who punish crime, perpetrate crime, and are victims of crime. Central to this study is the notion of deterrence, which is the extent to which PPAs prevent people from committing crime. The standard economic conception of deterrence is based on the assumption that individuals weigh up the gains to be made from committing crime versus the probability of being caught and the costs of punishment. Therefore increasing the likelihood of being caught and the severity of the penalties reduces the incentives to commit crime. A distinction is also made between general and specific deterrence. General deterrence refers to the effect of punishment on the general public (i.e., potential offenders). It is the indirect experience of punishment, such as observing or having knowledge of the punishment of others, that might deter individuals from committing crime. Specific deterrence refers to the effects of punishment on those who have experienced it (i.e., punished offenders). In this case, the pain of the direct experience of punishment is such that it deters future offending. Residents in West Belfast hold the belief that PPAs have a general deterrent effect on criminal behavior, that is, if PPAs did not exist more individuals would commit crime, and the crimes would be more serious. As evidence of this, they point to the relative absence of hard drugs, principally heroin and cocaine, in areas controlled by Republicans who have taken a strong stance against drugs and executed drug dealers. This is contrasted with Loyalist neighborhoods, where both these drugs are much more available. It is impossible to test the validity of PPAs having a general deterrent effect, but noting the existence of the belief is crucial to understanding why so many residents report incidents and individuals to the IRA in the full knowledge that these individuals may be violently attacked. Rather, this book focuses more closely on the puzzle as to why PPAs appear to have had a limited specific deterrent effect on the group of young people who have experienced them directly. That is, being beaten or shot has not prevented them from repeating the same type of offenses for which they had been punished.

The structure of the book is as follows. In chapter 1, I argue that from the early days of the political conflict in the 1970s the conditions were such that the IRA adopted some of the functions of the state, namely the provision of policing and punishment of ordinary crime. The hostility of the statutory criminal justice system, particularly the police, toward the working-class Catholic community dramatically increased the costs of using state services. The high levels of disaffection and aggression among working-class Catholics toward the police meant that the state could no longer fulfill its function and police the community in any "normal" way. A demand for policing therefore existed. Simultaneously, this demand was met and fostered by the IRA, which had the motivation, the manpower, and the monopoly on the use of violence necessary to carry out this role. As such, the somewhat systemic perpetration of PPAs by the IRA can be seen as a form of "extralegal governance" whereby the IRA provides the public good of policing and protection to the local population outside of the law.

Chapter 2 begins to address the core issue of the book, namely trying to understand the behavior of the hoods by examining their specific offense patterns. This chapter, which is based on the ethnographic data, shows that although the hoods' offending generally involves heightened physical risks, there is little financial reward for their endeavors, as, for example, in the case of joyriding, whereby most stolen cars are abandoned rather than sold on for profit. This book does not attempt to explain why some young people get involved in criminal behavior and others do not, but rather why delinquent young people in West Belfast engage in particular antisocial behaviors. This work, however, is based upon certain theoretical assumptions about the nature of delinquency.

Drawing upon the early traditions of Albert Cohen (1955) and Richard A. Cloward and Lloyd E. Ohlin (1960), the ethnographic data described in chapter 2 provides evidence that the hoods operate in a subculture of delinquency described by Cohen in his study "Delinquent Boys" as "a way of life that has somehow become traditional."[32] These sociologists studying offending among young people have provided two basic insights about juvenile delinquency: first, that it typically is not a solitary enterprise, but a group activity; and second, that delinquent activities, rather than being engaged in by biologically and psychologically abnormal individuals, typically develop in the sociological context of particular territorial locales and cultural traditions. In addition, it was recognized that delinquency took a number of forms and was engaged in for a variety of reasons.

The socially deterministic approach of Cohen and of Cloward and Ohlin was challenged by David Matza (1964), who began with the premise that analysis should start from the meanings that actors attribute to their actions in the world. He argued that the understandings people hold about their behavior are crucial to their behavior (whatever the accuracy of those understandings may be). Therefore, instead of viewing delinquents as compelled to misbehavior by social forces beyond their control, a better understanding of delinquency could come about once we begin to appreciate the purposes, motives, and fears that shape the delinquent action. Furthermore, delinquent and nondelinquent actions are understood in terms of the same general processes. Matza therefore "shifted the attention away from the creation of general behavioural predispositions to the microsocial contexts in which specific acts occur."[33]

Matza also challenged the view that there exists a delinquent subculture, suggesting instead a subculture of delinquency. He suggests that two general concepts regarding delinquency must be kept in mind: first, that there exists in society a frame of mind that encourages and allows its members to behave illegally and gain prestige from doing so; and second, that the subculture of delinquency remains basically committed to the important values of conventional culture. Matza argued that conventional culture is often complex and many-sided, featuring not just law-abiding morality but also hedonism, frivolity, and excitement. The delinquent is committed neither to the subculture of delinquency nor to the conventional culture. Instead, the delinquent chooses more-or-less consciously to "drift" between the one and the other, often many times during the course of a day.[34]

The dominant features of working-class culture are examined in chapter 3. In particular, the ways in which status and prestige can be gained among the adult male population, and the fact that the hoods are excluded from these paths to power, are explored. Chapter 3 also examines the relationships between the hoods and the influence of their friends and associates on their offending. Following Matza's assumptions, the analysis in this book is framed in terms of the understandings that both the hoods and ex-hoods either have or had of their antisocial behavior. Thus studying the world of the hoods in their own terms opened the way to an increased understanding of their behavior. In the process, the data revealed that rather than being anomic the hoods do adhere to a set of norms. The challenge remains to understand the hoods' subculture and make sense of their behaviors.

Chapter 4 attempts to get to the heart of the matter and tackles this puzzle: why doesn't the punishment administered by the paramilitaries and/or the state deter these young people from further recidivism? This lack of a specific deterrent effect violates the rational norm on which deterrence is founded, that certainty and severity of punishment will prevent reoffending, and has bewildered many local people, paramilitaries, criminal justice practitioners, and politicians for some time. The explanatory model proposed in chapter 4 is that of a signaling game whereby hoods engage in specific behaviors to prove their toughness and status to other hoods. The model, developed from economics, game theory, and biology,[35] explains why people engage in self-destructive behaviors in order to gain group acceptance: often the qualities they wish to display are hard to observe by others who are interested in them and can be easily mimicked by purely verbal claims.[36] In this instance, the hoods' participation in seemingly irrational antisocial behavior and their response to punishment amount to a set of signals that only the toughest among them can afford to display. I argue that the hoods attempt to distinguish the "really tough" from the "not so tough," the authentic from the inauthentic, through the process of being punished. The certainty and severity of repeated physical punishment will not deter the person who is really tough and therefore acts as a sorting signal.

Chapter 5 turns to the Protestant community and examines PPAs perpetrated by Loyalist paramilitaries. Although the violent methods used by Republican and Loyalist armed groups are similar, their motivation is somewhat different. In particular, the supply of PPAs carried out by

Loyalist paramilitaries outweighs the demand from the local population. In this case, PPAs are used against delinquent young people, but they are also used to discipline members and settle scores within and between groups to a greater extent than in the Republican case. Chapter 5 also examines antisocial behavior among young people in Protestant areas and finds differences between Protestants and Catholics in the specific types of offending. The explanation for this variation lies in the structure and number of Loyalist armed groups and the different types of opportunities for community recognition, which the respective political and paramilitary organizations offer to them.

The book concludes with a commentary on the changing political scene in Northern Ireland and reflects on the effect that these changes will have on the roles and functions of the various Republican and Loyalist paramilitary groups. As the number of PPAs diminishes, and the phenomenon perhaps ceases altogether, what effect will this have on the behavior of young people who, for so many years, have been victims of this violence?

ONE

West Belfast

This research was set in West Belfast, which contains the highest concentration of Catholics (82 percent) in Northern Ireland.[1] Although the West Belfast parliamentary constituency contains some Protestant wards, including the Loyalist Shankill area, to many outside the area, West Belfast means "Catholic West Belfast," an area bounded by the peace line—which is a wall that was erected in the 1970s to separate Catholics and Protestants who live in the neighborhoods that branch out from the Falls Road and the Shankill Road—and the M1 motorway, which stretches out to the Twinbrook and Poleglass developments in the Lisburn Borough Council area.

Approximately one-third of Belfast's population lives in this area,[2] which is characterized by high levels of economic inactivly, poverty, and ill health.[3] According to the Northern Ireland Multiple Deprivation Measure, West Belfast ranks as the most deprived parliamentary constituency in Northern Ireland on all measures except the Employment Scale (where it is ranked second-most deprived).[4] Although categorized as a working-class area, West Belfast comprises prosperous residents as well; while some leave their neighborhoods in search of larger houses and a more secure environment, others do stay. It is thus not completely homogeneous.

Since 1997 Sinn Féin has dominated the political landscape of West Belfast. In the 2005 Westminster General Elections, with a turn-out of 65 percent, Sinn Féin's leader, Gerry Adams, won the seat with a 70 percent share of the vote.[5] It is thus reasonable to describe West Belfast as a Nationalist and Republican area, and throughout the rest of this book it will be referred to as such. There are a number of other areas in Northern Ireland that are regarded as heartland communities of the Republican Movement. These include the Bogside and Creggan areas of Derry/Londonderry and the rural areas of South Armagh and mid-

Tyrone.[6] All have distinct characteristics, but West Belfast is by far the largest of the Republican areas in Northern Ireland. For the purpose of this book, West Belfast will refer to the Catholic wards in the West Belfast parliamentary constituency.

This description of West Belfast as a socially and economically deprived enclave does not differentiate it significantly from areas in other cities within the United Kingdom. Yet, according to the novelist Robert McLiam Wilson, "Under the circumstances, Belfast was a pretty famous place. When you considered that it was the under-populated capital of a minor province, the world seemed to know it excessively well."[7] Belfast has become notorious because it has been at the epicenter of political conflict for over three decades, and the streets and housing developments of West Belfast—the Falls Road, Divis Flats, Ballymurphy—have all become synonymous with the "Troubles," the euphemism used by people in Ireland to describe the conflict in Northern Ireland. Between July 1969 and February 2010, 3569 deaths and over 40,000 injuries have been directly linked to the conflict in Northern Ireland and West Belfast's present-day character has been forged in this political and civil unrest that has levied an immense toll on its residents.[8] Fifty-three percent of those who have been killed in the conflict were civilians, and West Belfast has borne a large proportion of this loss of life. Just over a third of all those who have died lived in five postal districts located in North and West Belfast.[9]

These shared experiences of poverty, deprivation, and conflict have helped to facilitate a strong in-group dynamic that has solidified and brought a degree of unity to those who live in West Belfast. This identification and display of a resolute wider community spirit does not mean that West Belfast is one cohesive and harmonious unit. Closer examination reveals a localism with strong allegiances within specific areas and neighborhoods such as Beechmount, Clonard, Springhill, and Ballymurphy. To a local person, the boundaries between these areas are clearly defined and obvious, but strangers can be forgiven for getting confused.

The association and cooperation among residents in the developments and streets of this predominantly working-class enclave is strong. There is a firm sense of neighborliness, a "kindly friendliness," among those who live in West Belfast.[10] Residents describe how well they know each other: "At night if you see anyone standin' at their door you'd get up and dander over and chat away, have a bit of craic and before you know it half the street is out. But, it's good that way, you can't move but everyone knows about it, but I'd rather have it like this than not knowin' who's next door" (Local Resident H). They provide examples of the practical support and help they give to one another: "Everyone around here gets on really well, and we do look out for each other. I collapsed one day in the house, and as soon as one person found out that there was something wrong, practically the whole street was in my house to see if I was all right" (Local Resident B).

Meetings about local issues are often attended by between 200 and 300 residents. Madeleine Leonard's inquiry into the informal economy in a housing development, called "Newbury" for the purposes of her study, found the community extremely cohesive: "[S]urvival strategies are collective rather than individual or household endeavours. Mutual inter-dependence exists between most inhabitants of the estate" she wrote.[11]

The population in West Belfast has remained fairly static since the early 1970s, when there was a large influx of Catholic "refugee" families who had been intimidated into leaving their homes in more religiously mixed neighborhoods. Seventy-five percent of Leonard's sample had lived in the Newbury development for over twenty years; 50 percent of the males between 26 and 40 years of age had been born in the development, as had 72 percent of the females in this age group.[12] One local resident recently described the limited mobility in West Belfast: "I know all my neighbours because they've all been here a long time, and it's all the same ones. I'm in this house nine years now, and I don't think anyone new has moved in since then. I only moved into this house from down the street and all the rest of them have been here for years" (Local Resident L).

Extended kinship networks, with generations of the same family living in close proximity, have also reinforced the localism, identification, and sense of belonging:

My ma and da still live in the house I was born in, and our Eileen got the house two doors up when she got married. Her husband's parents, they live two streets across and, when we got married, we moved in

here down the road a bit. It's great for the kids, because if somethin'
happened and we weren't here, they could just run up the road to my
ma's or our Eileen's. (Local Resident D)

In West Belfast, the term "community" proliferates. It is used to describe a cluster of residents, whose composition can range from all those
living in West Belfast to residents of one housing development, neighborhood, or street. While all residents share the unique history and experience of living in West Belfast, the notion that transforms a group
of individuals who live in close proximity to one another into a "community" is cooperation. This concept of "community," in the words of
Eric A. Posner, refers to "a group of people who engage in co-operative
relationships with each other, and who signal their type to each other by
taking actions whose salience results from common pasts, interests or
understandings."[13] In West Belfast this translates into action that mini-
mizes and often excludes any formal statutory involvement. Hence, a
"community response" is an informal cooperative response that is initi-
ated and orchestrated by local residents.

To muddy the waters further, the political connotations of the term
"community" vary. Sinn Féin activists organize local residents in cooperative responses to a wide range of issues with a vigor not seen among
the other political parties. The political emphasis of such collective action depends on the personalities involved and the issue at hand. Sometimes only those who wholeheartedly support Sinn Féin will endorse an
initiative, and on other occasions, the scheme will gain the backing of
a broader cross-section of residents. For example, organized "community" protests by residents against the Protestant Orange Order's annual
march up Springfield Road—a celebration of the military victory of the
Protestant King William III (William of Orange) over the Catholic King
James II at the Battle of the Boyne in 1690—are more overtly political
than protests held against joyriders. Conversely, there are times when the
term "community" is used without these political overtones, such as Féile
an Phobail (the West Belfast Festival). This annual event in August was
established to replace the partisan commemoration of Internment by cel-
ebrating and showcasing the West Belfast community's contribution to
the arts.[14]

The symbols that are on public display in West Belfast primarily express allegiance to Republican beliefs. Murals and posters adorn walls, depicting images of dead Republicans, paramilitary might and determination, and historical suffering at the hands of successive British governments. Flags—the green, white, and orange of the Irish tricolor[15]—flutter from the top of high-rise buildings and defiantly line the roads. At the entrance to the Poleglass development, for many years, a sign read, "You are now entering Republican West Belfast"; and in Milltown Cemetery, the site of Loyalist Michael Stone's televised gun attack,[16] memorials to dead Republicans killed in action are festooned with flowers. Thus, the observer is given the impression that the inhabitants of West Belfast subscribe to a collective set of values, including political, social, and cultural beliefs. The difficulties associated with surveying local attitudes, however, mean that there is a lack of evidence as to how strong and widespread this local consensus is.[17] Many residents do not consciously define their allegiances, and some may never declare themselves for or against certain factions in their neighborhood, striving instead to maintain the impression of cooperativeness, friendliness, and belonging.[18] Nevertheless, the public image presented by residents of West Belfast is one of a collective identity that is different from the rest of the population of Northern Ireland.

The West Belfast Economic Forum noted on its website that although internal perceptions of West Belfast, symbolized by graffiti that asserts "The West is the Best," are positive, the external view has often been very negative. The forum explains that in the media and in official arenas, "West Belfast" has become a pejorative code word for "Republican" and, more tangibly, "trouble." Such is the insinuation when newspapers report that "a West Belfast man was held for questioning," or when the police or British army ask a suspect, "Are you from the west of the city?"[19]

On the one hand, West Belfast is no more than a geographical location—the west of the city of Belfast. On the other hand, however, it is a powerful symbol of political and cultural identity forged during thirty-five years of severe social and economic problems and civil and political turmoil: in the words of the West Belfast Economic Forum, "it is an emblematic reference to a set of political beliefs, a culture, and a

'way of life.'"[20] An integral expression of this "way of life" is the reliance upon local cooperation to address issues and problems in the area, using resources and strategies that, in general, do not involve the state. This becomes increasingly evident when crime, policing, and punishment are examined in more detail.

The Demand for Informal Justice

West Belfast has a crime problem, the extent of which is unknown. Even the best aggregate data available used in the Noble Multiple Deprivation Measure, which incorporates Northern Ireland Fire Brigade data on malicious and deliberate fires and police incidence data on "disturbances" with reported crime data to construct a "Crime and Disorder" domain, must be viewed with some scepticism.[21] The following factors that influence the probability of an offense not being reported suggest that it is likely that a significant amount of crime in West Belfast remains unreported to the police.[22]

The socioeconomic characteristics of age, personal and household income, and labor-market status all affect reporting decisions. Older, higher-income, and employed people are more likely to have insured their property and are therefore more likely to report an incident, especially if it involves a loss.[23] In West Belfast, 28 percent of the population are under 16 years of age, and 49 percent of the population are economically inactive.[24] They are thus less likely to have insurance and are more likely to have been previous victims of crime, which is also correlated with not reporting.

Those who perceive the police to be ineffectual or who have had a negative experience with the police, such as being stopped and searched, and thus fear or distrust the police, will be less likely to report. Likewise, those who view the police as being an illegitimate force will be less prone to seek their help. Evidence from the Social Attitudes in Northern Ireland (1992) revealed that although the majority of Catholics would contact the police, it was political rather than religious affiliation that produced the greatest polarization. In addition, low-income and working-class respondents were less likely to contact the police than more middle-class respondents.[25] In working-class, Sinn Féin–dominated West Belfast it is therefore expected that reporting rates would be low.

Early in the fieldwork, a former prisoner used the term "policing vacuum" to summarize the policing problems in Northern Ireland. This was to become a familiar refrain both in interviews and in the literature, as Republicans have long argued that the informal paramilitary policing system has evolved to fill this law-and-order void. It has been argued, however, that with a state police force and a military together comprising over 30,000 members, as well as the policing activities of both Republican and Loyalist paramilitaries, it would be truer to say that there is a surfeit of policing in Northern Ireland, rather than a vacuum.[26] In effect, there is a lack of consensus as to how the population should be policed, and by whom. In Republican areas the conditions exist for the IRA to rival, if not to supplant, the state in the provision of policing and punishment. There are, however, a number of other solutions to the problems of crime in West Belfast.

Handling It Themselves

If local people do not go to the police, what do they do about crime in their area? There was some acceptance that, as with the disruption caused by political troubles or the summer Marching Season,[27] local people would simply have to put up with things and live with the disorder:

> To tell you the truth I just keep my head down and don't bother anyone because I don't want any bother. I just try and ignore the hoods and get on with things. People round here shout and scream and get on, but I think it just makes them lads worse, you know aggravates them, gets them going. (Local Resident B)

Residents try to find safe parking for their cars, and keep their children indoors at night. By keeping a low profile and taking precautions, they hope to avoid becoming victims of a criminal offense.

Others try to tackle the problem in ways that vary across the assortment of developments and neighborhoods, depending on the intensity of the problems and the personalities involved in the local decision-making process. Public meetings of up to 500 people, (sometimes organized by Sinn Féin, and sometimes not), have spawned locally implemented schemes, that invariably and crucially do not directly involve the state.

Before deciding to act collectively, residents may try to mediate in disputes between neighbors and offer advice as to appropriate agencies, social workers, or other sources of support that may be able to help them deal with problem cases. They may ask the parents of vandals or joyriders to assert some control over their child, who are all too often beyond the authority and influence of their parents. They may also attempt to divert delinquent young people into youth and community groups. There are scores of "politically nonaligned" individuals who play a role in dealing with the many problems in the locality.[28] One husband and wife organized a soccer team for the young people who live on their street. Every year they got funding from local businesses for new soccer jerseys, entered tournaments, and took their team away on day trips:

> There was nothin' for them to do, and they were just standin' at the corner of the street gettin' in people's way. I was walkin' past one day and said to them, "Have youse got nothin' better to do?" and they said "No." So, I went and got a ball and we all went down and had an old kick-about, and that's how it got started. Now they're mad for it, they love it. The parents use it as a threat as well. If they don't behave or do as they're told, they'll ring me up and I'll go down to the house and say, "I can't have anyone in my team who doesn't pull their weight and respect their ma and da." We have a laugh about it afterwards, but it really works. We keep in contact with them all. They come round the house and help out with the younger ones. And you know, they've all stayed in school and got their exams and then got jobs, none of them went into drugs or bad drinkin' or joyridin', some of them even trained with the local team. I'm really proud of all of them; they're all good kids. (Local Resident L)

Examples of more direct collective action include protest marches against joyriding and the removal of graffiti and rubbish scattered around the housing developments by joyriders.[29] Other initiatives involve the direct targeting of individuals like a "name and shame" and boycott campaign instigated by residents of the Glenkeen estate. Large placards were placed on lamp-posts and pillars around the development naming alleged petty offenders. Shops, taxi companies, pubs, and liquor stores were asked to refuse services to those identified as "thugs."[30]

VIGILANTES

In 1996 and 1997 groups of residents began to take a more robust stance against joyriders in particular. They placed boulders at the entrances of housing developments to keep cars from entering through the narrow walkways of these residential areas.[31] They also began patrolling their streets at night with walkie-talkies and hurley sticks[32] and attempted to impose a curfew on the large groups of young people who would congregate to watch the joyrider's race their cars.[33] They claimed to be "Neighborhood Watch" groups not vigilantes orchestrated by the Republican Movement.

> This has nothing to do with any political parties or any paramilitary organizations. We aren't vigilantes, this is the community working together to stamp out crime. People have just had enough. At the start, things were heated and people were doing stupid things, but now things have calmed down. We intend to do our best to curb joyriding, large crowds of youths standing about drinking, drug dealing and all sorts of antisocial behaviour going on. (Resident, Poleglass estate)[34]

In general Sinn Féin supported these initiatives but denied any role in organizing them: "[T]heir growth and presence is about ownership and defence of the community" (Sinn Féin Youth Worker H). In opposing the expulsion of families by Poleglass residents, Sinn Féin Councillor Annie Armstrong stated that although they opposed "undisciplined vigilantes," they would "endorse a well-disciplined and well-organised community-based watch."[35] Nevertheless, the aggressive stance, sense of mob rule, and the actual instances of violence associated with these groups left some interviewees skeptical about these claims:

> I've yet to see a distinction between paramilitaries and vigilantes, they work out from the centre and mix in the same social circles; it all gets very blurred as to who is who. The common perception is that they

are one and the same person. Their motivation is that they want to care and protect their own community but I would have a lot of difficulty with their methodology. (Community Worker Q)

Others thought that they were unrepresentative of the community and ineffective: "Women weren't allowed at the vigilante meeting in ___ Street. The vigilantes watch for joyriders. They don't necessarily set out to beat them up. It depends on the group, but they have no moral authority with the kids because they used to do the same thing when they were younger" (Shop Owner P).[36] As for the hoods, they called them "Rah [IRA] wannabes."

Most of the so-called Neighborhood Watch groups in West Belfast have been occasional and relatively disorganized. The one exception to this is Direct Action Against Drugs (DAAD), which emerged in 1994 and was responsible for the execution of 11 alleged drug dealers. It is generally assumed that DAAD was simply a flag of convenience for the IRA when it was constrained by the cease-fire and Sinn Féin's peace negotiations. Sinn Féin continued to deny any association between the two organizations but showed them tacit support:

In 1995 DAAD shot an ex-Republican prisoner. People didn't believe the accusation that he was importing drugs, but they wouldn't have shot him if it hadn't been true. There is a lot of speculation as to who they are. There is no evidence of a direct connection to anyone, but their organisation is probably in North Belfast. What is clear is that they are defending Nationalists. If it is Loyalists who are dealing drugs to fund their activities, then dealing drugs is a direct attack on the Nationalist community. (Sinn Féin Youth Worker H)

This statement refers to Francis 'Fra' Collins, former leader of the IRA in North Belfast, who was shot for alleged drug dealing. Fra's widow claimed that she ran after her husband's murderers shouting "Youse bastards!" to which they replied "Up the 'RA!"[37]

Given Sinn Féin and the IRA's dominance in West Belfast, it is unlikely that a violent vigilante group could operate in the area without their knowledge and sanction, if not their direct cooperation. DAAD's relative longevity of four years or so suggests the IRA's ease with its shows of strength and implies that the two organizations are closely linked. By contrast, the less well-organized and more transient nature of some of the other vigilante groups suggests that they have received less support from the formal administration of the IRA and "sometimes, as the Republican Movement [has] found out, vigilantes tend to be a law unto themselves" (Ex-prisoner F). Individual Republicans might get involved without the endorsement of the organization. In 1996, the IRA was blamed for the attack on 18-year-old Martin Doherty, who was gagged and had steel spikes driven into his arms and legs. The IRA in a call to the *Irish News* claimed local people were responsible but admitted that "there may have been Republican involvement because of the area [Turf Lodge] where the beating took place."[38]

The origins and political allegiances of members of the various vigilante groups may be uncertain, but their existence is evidence of the culture of informality that emphasizes taking care of things locally without state intervention, and of a demand for the use of strong-arm techniques.

SUPPORT FOR THE IRA

The IRA's contemporary policing role emerged from the political and civil unrest in the late 1960s and early 1970s. Growing discontent among the Catholic population in Northern Ireland came to a head with the Civil Rights Movement in 1969, which was violently opposed by militant Protestants.[39] Civil Rights protests were attacked by Protestant mobs and by families from both religions who lived in the "wrong districts" and had been intimidated and forcibly evicted from their homes. The Scarman Report (1972) on the violence and civil disturbances of 1969 concluded that five times as many Catholics were forced out of their homes as Protestants, and many of those Catholic families sought refuge in West Belfast. The British army was brought in to help keep the peace, but the situation deteriorated.

The traumatic psychological effect of this period of intense sectarian violence and civil disturbance on the population of West Belfast has been immense. Accounts of this time describe the perils of a trip to the corner shop as sniper bullets ricocheted off alley-way walls; the dangers of walking home from the pub late at night with Loyalist assassins looking for a Catholic victim; violent confrontations with the British army and the police firing CS gas and, later, plastic bullets; petrol bombs being thrown through the windows of homes. It was impossible to live in any of West Belfast's neighborhoods and not experience firsthand the indiscriminate and terrifying violence. It was this and the heavy-handed techniques of the police and army that forged strong allegiances to the IRA, despite that organization's flaws. Fionnuala O'Connor quotes an adult education teacher in West Belfast who explains that outsiders who would condemn such support of an organization that uses violence are dismissed as

> people who live somewhere nice, who don't know what it is to have their front door kicked down, who haven't had members of their family shot dead . . . Then there are the people who say, "I wouldn't do it myself—but I have nonetheless a deep sympathy with those who do it, and with what they suffer as a result . . . I wouldn't do those things, but you can't abandon those who do, they're part of us."[40]

The price of loyalty to the IRA has been high. It has been suggested that defending Catholics by embarking on an offensive campaign against the British army and the police succeeded in endangering Catholics further by drawing them into violent conflict and deepening sectarian divisions.[41] Republican paramilitaries have been responsible for the deaths of over 25 percent of all Catholics killed during the Troubles.[42] But it is this early period of the Troubles that helps to explain why, despite the costs, the IRA retained such strong support in West Belfast. The belief remains that without the IRA, Catholics would have been even more exposed and vulnerable to attack from all quarters.

Gauging the level of support for the various paramilitary groups and their use of violence in Northern Ireland is very problematic. Bernadette Hayes and Ian McAllister note that respondents in public opinion surveys are reluctant to admit their support, which in any case is often dependent on the particular circumstances at the time they are asked the questions. Nonetheless, using data from the 1999 Northern Ireland and Republic of Ireland European Values Study, they found that 26 percent of respondents in Northern Ireland expressed some level of sympathy for Republican paramilitaries and an almost identical figure of 27 percent of respondents sympathized with Loyalist paramilitaries. Furthermore, 42 percent of Catholics were sympathetic toward Republican paramilitaries as compared to 24 percent of Protestants who expressed sympathy for Loyalist paramilitaries.[43]

Members of Sinn Féin and the IRA are also residents of West Belfast; they have jobs, families, and sporting interests, and their neighbors do not separate them from other, less obviously politically aligned, residents. Those who live outside of the area often simplify support for Republicans into black-and-white "always yes" or "always no" categories. The reality is that residents are driven by a mixture of motives and concerns, which permeates attitudes and backing for both organizations. As one of those interviewed by O'Connor put it, "People don't necessarily have a line on the IRA that they can trot out. . . . Many don't consciously work something out, they don't separate the IRA off as a phenomenon—it's part of their circumstances."[44]

If support for the IRA in general fluctuates, so does particular support for the IRA's involvement in, and methods of, crime control. Thus, "Mrs. McBride, who called in 'the lads' [the IRA] to deal with a break-in at her home or a mugging, might object if Mrs. McCann's son was beaten up by hooded men with hurley sticks the next night."[45] Frank Burton and Jeffrey A. Sluka in studies of West Belfast that were ten years apart also argued that there was a great deal of ambivalence among residents regarding PPAs.[46]

Interview evidence suggests a complex picture. Community Worker R had little sympathy with the victims of PPAs: "Look, the way I see it, the paramilitaries give people as much of a chance as possible. But at the end of the day, if they don't take that chance and stop, then they have to take the consequences. I mean, if I stick my hand in the fire then I'll get burnt—right?" There were even complaints that the IRA was not harsh enough. When masked men claiming to be from the IRA told Father Joseph Quinn that four teenagers would be shot unless they left Ireland within 24 hours, there was widespread political condemnation of the expulsions. However, Father Quinn expressed surprise at local reaction to the death threats to the four young men: "The reaction when the news broke in the community, from what I hear on the ground, was that it was overdue," he said.[47]

Residents were faced with a lack of alternatives—"Nobody does it [policing] fairly," remarked Community Worker G. According to Community Worker S, "[T]he community just abdicates their responsibility to the paramilitaries, and do something that doesn't work. Physical force is the only option that they feel they have open to them, and if you're not up to it yourself, then you get someone else to do it for you." A case worker with Base 2, an organization that helps those threatened by the paramilitaries, broadly agreed with this view. He said, "It's a very selective group of people who are subjected to the violence, so it's easy for the community to support it. In a way, although [the violence is] very close, they are also very distanced from it, and [they think] it's not going to happen to them." Community Worker G, however, saw the acceptance of violence simply as a case of people being weary of the problems in their neighborhoods:

> They don't see anything else working, and so they will go for punishment. There is definitely a strong punishment orientation in the community and not going to report to the police, it has become normalised. Some would say that they are wrong but they are trapped, what can they do? It's not realistic to move out of the area. I have met people who are more against it than they are for it, but they feel powerless to do anything about it.

Unionist politicians argue that the IRA exercises such a high level of social control in West Belfast that residents live in abject fear of them. Support for the IRA is, in their opinion, based on an unwillingness to raise one's head above the parapet and express any form of dissent. Alternatively, Sluka contends that the kind of social control that inhibits the expression of divergent views in West Belfast on issues such as policing is not its domination by the IRA but rather community or peer pressure. He argues that someone who lives in a neighborhood where people hold strong and fairly homogeneous political views and who expresses a view that differs radically from group norms, values, and expectations, is likely to experience group pressure.[48]

Undoubtedly, some residents in West Belfast do display false preferences regarding the IRA's policing and punishment role. That is, in response to real or imagined social pressure, they convey a preference that they do not necessarily hold. In conversation with their neighbors they either publicly support or consent to the IRA's actions, while privately disagreeing with the intervention, or, more commonly, they refrain from public dissent, thereby signaling consent: "A lot of people are afraid to speak their own mind. People don't speak what they're thinking. People keep their heads down, as long as it [the violence] doesn't happen to me" (Local Resident M). Local Resident B described how one evening the IRA

> took over the house opposite to do [shoot] a wee lad. Don't get me wrong, he had it comin', he was a right terror. Anyway you should have heard the squeals of him; the whole street heard it and came out to see what was happenin'. The fella across the road was full [drunk] and started shoutin', "murderin' bastards, go fuck yourselves you fuckin' cowards" and stuff like that, really making a racket. This other man who lives on up the street walked over to him and tapped him on the shoulder. He just told him to mind his own business and be quiet and go to bed and he just shut up.

This incident provokes a number of observations. First, the respondent neither condoned nor condemned the attack. He may have felt that the victim of the attack had behaved in such a way as to provoke physical punishment, or he may have believed the attack was uncalled for, but he never publicly stated his preference. Second, although the drunk very publicly stated his opinion in the first instance, the "tap on the shoulder" silenced him. It is not known whether the man who silenced him had any connections with the IRA. Therefore, it is not possible to identify whether his intervention was a threat from the IRA ("be quiet, or else"), or an exertion of social pressure from the neighborhood ("be quiet, because this is the way things are done around here"), or even a friendly warning ("be quiet, or else you could be in danger"). By keeping quiet and walking away, the drunk calculated that it was no longer in his interests to voice his dissent. He thus acquiesced with the general consensus among the local residents to "keep quiet" and, in this instance, comply with the IRA's actions.

The phenomenon of this silence is reflected in a comparison of IRA and Loyalist attacks: IRA punishment squads are found more likely to be larger and more likely to punish several victims at once, and their attacks are 50 percent more likely to be witnessed by unharmed observers than those perpetrated by Loyalists. Yet Loyalists are more likely to be tried and convicted of offenses related to PPAs.[49] The IRA is less concerned with victim resistance and has greater confidence that witnesses will not give evidence against them.

The Supply of Informal Justice

The notion of an alternative system of justice coexisting alongside the colonial or statutory law-and-order process has long been a companion to resistance to British rule in Ireland. Republicans point to the tradition of informal justice in the eighteenth century and, in particular, the Dail Courts in the 1920s in the west of Ireland.[50] Paddy Hillyard[51] and Ronnie Munck[52] have argued that the alternative system of justice must be sited "within the broader context of a popular struggle," which, for Republicans, has extended throughout eight centuries of English occupation in Ireland.[53]

When the political crisis erupted in 1969, the IRA was a marginal organization, divided between Dublin-based advocates of a political program and activists who were keen to take up arms in response to the crisis in the north. The IRA reported that, at that time, the Republican Movement had ten guns in the whole of Northern Ireland.[54] It was extremely ill equipped to challenge Loyalists and the security forces, and the words "IRA equals I Ran Away" appeared on walls in West Belfast.[55] Within one year, the Dublin leadership had lost control of the northern pugilists. The movement split into the Official IRA (with Official Sinn Féin, later the Worker's Party, as its political wing), which was publicly opposed to the armed struggle, and the new Provisional IRA (PIRA: with Provisional Sinn Féin, later just Sinn Féin, as its political wing), which was mobilizing fast and mounting its military operation.

One of the first defensive steps taken by residents in West Belfast was to erect and man barricades to keep Loyalists out. Neighborhoods like Ballymurphy were declared "no-go areas" for the police and British army, which were accused either of standing by when Loyalists attacked nationalists or of being the aggressors themselves. Behind the barricades, the community organized itself. Refugee families were registered, accommodated, and fed. Links with other nationalist areas were established, and Central Citizen Defence Committees (CCDC) were set up to coordinate foot and car patrols and to supervise the barricades.[56] As a consequence of being the armed personnel on the streets, they also started to take responsibility for policing. The leadership of the CCDC was predominantly middle class, and eventually it became alienated from the working-class residents of West Belfast.[57] The so-called "People's Army" supplemented the CCDC's attempt at popular policing. This initiative was developed by a group of Catholic ex-service men after the introduction of Internment in 1971.[58] They were largely unarmed and claimed to be able to draw upon 8,000 men. However they, too, did not last long. The short-lived CCDCs and People's Army were joined by a series of Street Committees. These, too, were temporary, and they were soon overtaken by another initiative: policing by the IRA.

The IRA demonstrated right from the beginning that they were willing and able to take on this additional role. Crime was considered "anti-people," and as early as 1970 their repertoire of punishment included tarring and feathering, community service, exclusion, and imprisonment in a "jail" located in an electricity substation in Springhill. In November of that year they shot dead Arthur McKenna and Alexander McVicker, two local gangsters involved in organized crime.[59] Staunchly Republican Ballymurphy was particularly incendiary and characterized by recurrent and wholesale rioting throughout 1970. The IRA admitted that they found it difficult to control the rioting, and in January 1971 they even went so far as to place the more exuberant rioters under armed arrest. They told the British army, "If you get out of Ballymurphy, we can control it without your assistance."[60] This spate of rioting stopped most probably due to a combination of the IRA's influence and fatigue on the part of the rioters.

By mid-1974, the IRA was publicly announcing its intention to enforce more everyday rules, like speeding restrictions, to maintain public order.[61] Before long, they were also making statements about petty crime, and making pleas to parents to control their children but adding that "it is the whole community who suffers from these antisocial actions; that those responsible are members of that community, and so it is the community who should impose the sanctions."[62] By October 1976, the message had become unequivocal. There were no longer any attempts to negotiate with offenders or offer parents the opportunity to intervene. A notice in the *Ballymurphy News* read, "The Republican Movement reiterates previous warnings: ANYONE found to be joyriding and/or driving while drunk will be dealt with. We have more than enough problems on our streets without adding to them persons unfit to drive."[63]

The provision of protection from the external threat posed by Loyalists and the security forces, and from the internal threat created by neighborhood law-breakers, fused the IRA's military and civil roles together in the minds of local people. This relationship was cemented by the opening of seven Incident Centres in 1975. Originally established by the government to monitor earlier breaches of the 1975 cease-fire, the Incident Centres were staffed by Sinn Féin and offered assistance to those being attacked by Loyalists or experiencing problems with crime and antisocial behavior. When the cease-fire ended, the government withdrew its support of the Centres, but they remained as Sinn Féin offices where residents continued to report incidents of crime, and the IRA responded. In 1975, residents reported that people were being kneecapped on an almost weekly basis in the Upper Springfield area of West Belfast and, by the end of October 1975, a total of 374 punishment shootings had been recorded since the beginning of 1973.[64]

Other opportunities also existed to report crime. Individual Republicans received direct complaints: "[I]n every area there is a known Republican, a 'figurehead' if you want . . . who people could go to if they had a problem and didn't want to go to the police" (Ex-prisoner E). Certain bars and clubs provided an informal venue for residents to meet with Republicans. The Felons Club, where membership is reserved for ex-political prisoners, is popular with Sinn Féin and IRA members. It is a place where, over a pint, problems are raised, solutions are discussed, and decisions are taken as to whether an investigation should follow a complaint.

In the early 1970s, the IRA concluded that if it were to police effectively, it would have to establish a separate policing unit within the organization, and this became known as the civil administration: "People would report incidents to Sinn Féin first of all in the various centres, and they would be passed on, if necessary, to the civil administration and [it] would investigate the incident" (Ex-prisoner E).

The civil administration panels comprised Republicans whose sole responsibility was to adjudicate complaints from local people about criminal activity and individuals. The panels questioned complainants and witnesses until they had enough evidence to identify a suspect, who was then told to report at a prearranged time and place to be taken to an interrogation site, often an IRA safe house. If the suspect failed to report voluntarily, the IRA sought him out. One respondent described how over the years, the civil administration became more sophisticated, thorough, and accountable:

> You can imagine, the initial investigation was pretty basic, wasn't very thorough, and did lead to mistakes happening, and people were punished for the wrong things. . . . As I said the investigations were basic, so as people got experienced and different thoughts were put into it, for example, there was no use one person doing an investigation by themselves, there had to be two people to do that, so there could be no accusations of 'you said that' . . . there was always someone there who could corroborate what was said so as to make it more accountable. (Ex-prisoner E)

The IRA's questioning and interrogation methods have also modified over time:

> [I]f there was a case where someone said, "My house was burgled by such and such," they would go and get such and such and interrogate them. They [the IRA] didn't use very subtle methods of interrogation either because of the inexperience, the lack of knowledge about how to deal with it. So it was something that they didn't have the resources to deal with." (Ex-prisoner F)

The increased use of sophisticated security equipment like Close Circuit Television (CCTV) and security cameras has helped this process. When Danny (age 24) and Mark (age 19) robbed a news store, they first bought cigarettes and then returned to try and steal the contents of the cash register. They were filmed by the premises' CCTV camera, and the owner gave the videotape to Sinn Féin. When interrogated, Danny and Mark vehemently denied the robbery until the videotape was played. They were still wearing the same clothes as when they were filmed, and were instantly recognizable. Danny and Mark's previous record of joyriding, vandalism, and drug taking combined with their refusal to admit their guilt and accept responsibility for the offense resulted in an initial sentence of kneecapping. They would have been shot if it were not for the intervention of a community worker who succeeded in getting their sentence reduced to exclusion from Belfast.

The IRA does not have video evidence to aid every investigation. Its enforcers believe their information about suspects is reasonably accurate, but they are dogged by questions of accountability, particularly during the interrogation stage. Many victims claim to be innocent and unfairly punished: "[A]fter the shootings young people would say their confession was forced or they didn't say it at all" (Ex-prisoner E). Although Sinn Féin and the IRA have admitted to mistakes in the past, they are resolute that "[n]ot everyone who was shot was as innocent of the crime they had been accused of as they would like to claim" (Ex-prisoner E).[65] In response to allegations of coerced or falsified confessions, Ex-prisoner E reports that the IRA introduced the practice of tape-recording their interviews "so at the end of the day people couldn't come back and say, 'I didn't say that, you must be wrong' [without the IRA replying] 'Well, there was a tape recording of it, so why did you say it then?'" Despite this, many of the punishment victims continue to protest their innocence, and there have been clear examples of PPAs being used to settle personal grudges and also of cases of mistaken identity. Tommy (age 23) claimed that one of the punishment beatings he received, which hospitalised him for two weeks, was an act of revenge. He was involved in a fight with two other young men outside a club: "Everyone was drunk or high or both, and somebody said somethin' to somebody else, and then somebody threw a punch." According to Tommy, his opponents were involved with Sinn Féin, and one was the son of a senior Republican. His punishment beating was retaliation because of the fight. Following a quarrel with a senior Republican in a bar, Andrew Kearney was shot in both legs and left to bleed to death. His killers ripped out the telephone lines and jammed the lift to his flat preventing him from getting medical help.[66] John Brown, age 79, was beaten around the head and shot in both knees and ankles by Republican paramilitaries. His attackers misread the address they had been given and went to the wrong flat.[67]

According to official Republican protocol, sentencing usually follows investigation and interrogation. In the early days of the Troubles, when the IRA was much less organized and disciplined, decisions about punishment shootings could be made at a local level and were more arbitrary: "Men were shot for disobeying orders, sleeping with the wife of a man imprisoned for the cause, or for having disagreements with Provos and their families."[68] In order to improve consistency and accountability, the IRA specifically established small groups or cells in each area that operated under a control command: "The decisions in Belfast were never left to individuals or individual areas, they had to be verified and ratified, and any action taken had to be agreed upon before anything was done" (Ex-prisoner E). This system encompassed all IRA punishments, even for lesser crimes: "[I]f there has to be punishment or exclusion, it has to go to a higher level, it can't be done at a lower level. Certainly, they can recommend and they will be listened to, but it isn't their decision, it's at a higher level at that stage" (Ex-prisoner E).

Once the interrogation is over, and the IRA has obtained a confession or the investigation has convinced them of the suspect's guilt, the civil administration panel sentences the offender. All known previous offenses and punishments are taken into account and a history of persistent offending and/or previous punishment often results in a more severe sentence than for a first offense. For example, if an offense is drink-related, the panel may impose a boycott: "[H]e [the offender] won't be allowed to be served in local pubs; all the pubs will be visited and told not to serve him."[69] These boycotts are upheld by landlords and policed by the IRA.

Other factors are also taken into account. A respondent spoke of how some members of the sentencing panel in West Belfast brought their knowledge and experience from their "legitimate" roles as professional and voluntary youth and community workers to bear. In a number of cases the young people being sentenced had participated in youth and community programs run either by members or close associates of the panel, and sometimes funded by statutory agencies. Reports were presented about each young person's attendance in these programs, and evidence of positive participation was considered. One respondent described the decision not to physically punish one young person in order to enable him to attend an upcoming residential program designed to challenge his offending behavior. The panel also decided to postpone excluding him until they had received an evaluation of his participation in the course. If this report was positive, then he would be given a second chance; if negative, then he would be excluded. This is one example of the many intersections between the broader statutory criminal justice system, the informal system, and voluntary organizations.

In the 1970s, the Republican Movement attempted to make their policing role more accountable and community centered by establishing local 'People's Courts' in a number of areas. In each locality, a panel heard criminal cases, including rape, and decided disputes. The standard sentence was usually some form of community service.[70] These courts did not survive very long. Although they were intended to involve a large cross-section of residents, members of Sinn Féin and the IRA primarily operated them, and thus they were never wholly representative of the area.[71] A People's Court' system could function only if a significantly large section of the population in the localities gave its full commitment to the popular form of justice, and this political transformation did not take place.[72] Furthermore, according to Ex-prisoner E, "[T]he Community or People's Courts weren't very successful because the people who took part in them were constantly at risk of being arrested and prosecuted by the police, and there was also the threat of retaliation from those who were convicted." Although the People's Court system dissolved, the IRA, whose support, strength, and reputation for violence immunized its members from retaliation, continued to operate an informal system, investigating crimes and sanctioning offenders.

In addition to tackling crime, the IRA was concerned about informers in their midst. They wanted to keep locals away from the security forces and punished betrayal with death. According to Malcolm Sutton's index of deaths in the conflict in Ireland between 1969 and 2001, the first person to be murdered by the IRA as an alleged informer was 50-year-old William Bonner on October 2, 1972. He was shot in the Grosvenor Homing Pigeon's Club just off the Falls Road. Sutton identified sixty alleged informers killed by the IRA, who represent 3 percent of all those killed by the organization. Twenty-three (38 percent) of those shot for this crime were killed in West Belfast. These included 15-year-old Bernard Taggart, whose body was found on November 12, 1973. A placard was pinned to his chest; it read "tout."[73]

The Provisional IRA was not the only group policing in West Belfast. Rival Republican groups like the Official IRA, who had publicly eschewed the armed struggle, policed its own supporters.[74] The Irish National Liberation Army (INLA) formed in 1974 as a break-away group from the Officials and also took its turn at law enforcement. The INLA was prone to internal feuding, and so a proportion of its punishment activity may have been the settling of disputes between members. The Provisional IRA used the language of policing to discredit its rivals, referring to them as a "hoodlum element" and attacking them while all the time buttressing its own authority.[75] Despite all of this activity, official data suggest that between 1973 and 1987 the number of military-style killings by the Republican paramilitaries was typically higher than the number of civilian punishment shootings. The numbers of punishment attacks during this time are almost certainly underreported, although it is impossible to estimate to what degree. Nonetheless, it is clear that the insurgency remained the IRA's primary activity.

Nonviolent Methods

While the informal justice system in West Belfast is known best for the violence and brutality of PPAs, according to one respondent, "[W]ithin the Republican Movement the trend is to get away from the violence" (Ex-prisoner E). In 1999, Martin McGuinness stated this commitment "to develop alternative approaches which will make punishment attacks a thing of the past." He added, "Sinn Féin is totally opposed to punishment attacks. Those of us who genuinely want punishment attacks to end are engaged in the development of real alternatives."[76]

In the years prior to this statement, Sinn Féin explored numerous nonviolent approaches to the crime problem. In 1982, they issued a statement arguing for a "constructive alternative" for those offenders who were not engaged in hard-core crimes. This would involve a public commitment from the offender and a written undertaking to the IRA not to get reinvolved in criminal activity. The aim of this scheme was to end physical punishment and give offenders, "an opportunity to stop what they were doing. At the same time, they would have to deal with the consequences of their behaviour by facing the community concerned."[77] In a series of public meetings this initiative and a number of other nonviolent schemes were explored:

> There was a conscious decision taken even then to see what programmes were out there, and if we can refer people to them, let's do it, instead of actually curfewing them or whatever, excluding them . . . let's see if someone can work with them. So from then the decision was made to actually reduce the level of punishment beatings where possible by the Republican movement, but I think if you look back on it, I'm not sure that statistics on punishments will reflect that . . . there was a reduction over that period. That was them [Sinn Féin and the IRA] consciously saying we need to do something else here, this isn't working, let's find other alternatives—and hence the things that are going on in West Belfast now, with the different programmes. (Ex-prisoner F)

Many young offenders, however, interpreted these nonviolent initiatives as the IRA relaxing its policy toward crime. Public commitments to stop offending made by persistent offenders in a social club carried little sincerity. By 1984, letters were appearing in the Republican press arguing that "it is time the kid-gloves were taken off and the problem of the hoods removed."[78] One critic of the IRA's more liberal policy argued, "It must be blatantly obvious that there has been no substantial change of attitude by the hoods, nor is there likely to be in the foreseeable future."[79]

By restricting the police's capacity to operate in Republican areas, the IRA created the conditions under which their own capacity for military-style action and for internal security within their support communities was maximized, while inhibiting those of the state's security forces.[80] Since the cease-fires in the 1990s, it has become less important to keep the police out of areas for security reasons, than it has been to present them consistently as being inadequate, ineffective, and illegitimate. Thus, since 1996, Sinn Féin has explored many more nonviolent alternatives to state policing, including supporting Community Restorative Justice projects that were established on the back of the Good Friday Agreement

in 1998 and wider discussions on policing in Northern Ireland that cul-
minated in the Patten Report. The restorative justice initiatives were well
received by local residents, some of whom became volunteers, but, in the
beginning, the threat of violence toward offenders loomed in the background: "It will be made clear to young people on the scheme that if they
mess up then there will be consequences," one Restorative Justice volunteer said. The project now provides National Vocational Qualification
(NVQ) training to its volunteers and has dealt with over 1600 cases, but it
remains controversial because of the presence of ex-Republican prisoners
(between 10 and 25 percent of the volunteers are former prisoners) and
its reluctance to cooperate directly with the police.

The 1996 cease-fires and Sinn Féin's direct involvement in negotiations
with the British and Irish governments from September 1997 brought
about a sea-change in the attitude and behavior of Republicans regarding
policing. As figure 1 shows, this has manifested itself in a decrease in the
numbers of PPAs in recent years. Following Sinn Féin and the IRA's lead,
the political wing of the INLA, the Irish Republican Socialist Party (IRSP),
dissociated itself from violent methods.[81]

There have been other more subtle changes. Since the 1996 cease-fires
the IRA have become increasingly reluctant to use guns, and their preferred method of punishment has been some form of assault. Most dramatically, in 1995, in the lead-up to the cease-fire, there were no punishment shootings attributed to Republicans, but there were 141 recorded
assaults (see figure 1). As the political process has edged toward fully
devolved power-sharing in Northern Ireland, which is to include policing
and criminal justice, PPAs have steadily decreased. Sinn Féin's acceptance
of the reformed police service should herald the end of the so-called "policing vacuum" and with it the end of the informal system.

Extralegal Governance

Hillyard has argued that "the various forms of popular justice . . . in
Ireland have been characterised by the threat they pose to authority."[82]
While he considers the street committees of the early 1970s not to have

usurped any "significant element of power from the state,"[83] the question remains as to whether the IRA, through policing, achieved a form of extralegal governance.

In 1962, the liberal economist Milton Friedman succinctly summed up the basic functions of government as being "to protect our freedom from both the enemies outside our gates and from our fellow-citizens: to preserve law and order, to enforce private contracts, to foster competitive markets."[84] Avinash Dixit (2004) and others have argued that if the government institutions are unable or unwilling to perform these functions, then alternative modes of governance will arise.[85] Even in modern states with well-functioning governments, private security firms, bouncers at nightclubs, neighborhood watch programs, and gated communities with private guards all offer private protection replacing or supplementing official policing.[86] Diego Gambetta (1993) has shown that where the state is weak there is a higher risk that organized crime groups and mafias will emerge whose functions of policing, regulation of entry into a given market, dispute resolution, and taxation mirrors those of the government. Citing empirical cases in Sicily, Russia, Japan, New York, Chicago, and Hong Kong, Federico Varese lists ways in which these groups have paralleled state action and provided protection outside of the law to both the mainstream and underworld. These are "protection against extortion; protection against theft and police harassment; protection of thieves; protection in relation to informally obtained credit and the retrieval of loans; elimination of competitors; intimidation of customers, workers, and trade unionists for the benefit of employers; intimidation of lawful right-holders; and the settlement of a variety of disputes."[87] Two conditions are crucial to the rise of private protection: either illegal markets exist and transactions in these markets fall outside the jurisdiction of the state (as in the period between 1920 and 1933 during the Prohibition Era in the United States); or the state is unable to provide protection as a public good within its national borders (Sicily, the former Soviet Union, and Japan).[88] It is the latter condition that has the most bearing on the case of the IRA. In Northern Ireland, where the rule of law has been contested, private protection in the form of policing, the administration of punishment, and dispute resolution by armed groups has arisen. The costs to the local population of using the formal criminal justice system and the supply of manpower willing to perpetrate the necessary violence are key to understanding the development and continuation of this system of extralegal governance.

Costs

Dixit points out very clearly that even in countries with well-functioning legal systems, obtaining and enforcing a judgment in the court system can take a long time.[89] In the United Kingdom, the average length of time from the arrest of a persistent young offender to sentence jointly in the Crown Court and Magistrates Courts between January 2005 and March 2005 was sixty-six days.[90] This, of course, does not take into account the length of time between the offense being committed and the arrest of a suspect.

This general problem of timeliness has been exacerbated in West Belfast, where the police have been wary of responding to calls regarding ordinary crime or other matters unrelated to security or public order. Fearing an ambush, they first try to ascertain whether the call is genuine or is a setup, and this has led to a variable response time. One resident described how she phoned the police to report two joyriders racing around the local cemetery: "Forty-five minutes later they turn up: two Land Rovers and two army Land Rovers. By the time they got there, the wee lads had left the cars and run off. It wasn't worth the money it took to call the police in the first place" (Local Resident M). Since the peace process began in the mid-1990s, the threat to the police from a paramilitary group has decreased significantly, but there is still a reasonable probability that police presence will spark verbal taunts and violence. According to Community Worker Q, young people hate the police: "[T]hey throw stones at them and they call them names." While the police may consider the length of the response time to be positively related to the risks (that is, the higher the risk, the longer it takes to respond), residents either consider the risks to be lower or that the police should be impervious to the risk, and so in their minds the response times should be shorter.

A further cost to reporting to the police is the fear and suspicion felt by residents toward the police and the fear of reprisal from the IRA. There have been numerous allegations about, and investigations into, police misconduct toward the Catholic populace throughout period of the Troubles. The shadow of Internment still lingers. In 1978, the European Court of Human Rights ruled that the use of rough interrogation techniques in Northern Ireland constituted "inhuman and degrading punishment."[91] Tim Pat Coogan describes how "the army quite often simply picked up the wrong people, a son for a father, the wrong 'man with a beard living at No. 47' and so on. But by the time they were released, a number had suffered quite brutal treatment. . . . Internees were beaten with batons, kicked and forced to run the gauntlet between lines of club-wielding soldiers."[92] One respondent and his brother said that they were so badly beaten around the face while being questioned in police custody that, upon their release, they did not recognize each other. This respondent would not report a crime to the police because "once they have you, they can do what they like with you" (Local Resident N). These experiences led to the view expressed by Community Worker C that "to be honest, any Republican-minded person just wouldn't see it [going to the police] as an option."

The fear and suspicion that clouds interactions between the police and residents can distort perceptions of what exactly is happening in any given situation with a member of the public. Ronald Weitzer argues that it is possible that the long history of emergency legislation and counterinsurgency policing has contaminated assumptions and perceptions of ordinary law enforcement to the point where there is a degree of sectarian overdetermination toward even the most mundane encounters.[93] Thus, a night-time patrol to distribute parking tickets was described as an "under-cover-of-darkness operation" in the *Andersonstown News*.[94] Residents, like Community Worker S, referred to incidents when the police used ordinary encounters as an opportunity to deploy counterinsurgency tactics:

> My personal interactions have been satisfactory and at times generous. I got caught driving without tax and insurance and then was asked to be a tout for information. . . . What he said to me was, "If you ever have any information that can save a life, give me ring." There was no backlash and, of course, I never rang them. I was disappointed

because up until that point I was genuinely impressed by the way they were dealing with me, and then I just felt disgusted.

During the 1980s, the much-publicized "supergrass" trials reinforced the additional fear among residents that if they were seen calling the police, they might be thought of as informers or "touts."[95] A study on attitudes toward the criminal justice system in 2000 found that the fear of being labeled an informer and any subsequent reprisal from the paramilitary groups acted as a strong deterrent to contacting the police in Catholic/nationalist areas.[96] One resident described the police coming to her house:

> This fella gave my address as his address when he got out of prison. He must have done somethin' else because next thing I know, the peelers [police] are swarmin' all over my house. I came home and there were three Land Rovers outside my house, and the plain clothed ones [CID] were there as well. I swear to God I was shakin' like a leaf. Well, at first I thought he [my husband] was dead. I could see they [the police] didn't believe me when I said I'd never heard of the fella they were lookin' for . . . I was dead worried about what other people would think. All the street was out lookin' over here with me trying to tell the police I knew nothin' . . . After they went away I was tryin' to tell everyone that it was a mistake, you know, nothin' to do with me. Then she [a neighbour] said, "you shouldn't have let him walk across your door with his hat on." I was so panicked I never even thought. And then because they [the police] didn't believe me, they came back three times. I was shitting myself in case I was gonna get done. (Local Resident B)

This concern about what the neighbors would think about the presence of the police was repeated many times. Another resident's brother lived beside a derelict house where a lot of hoods were hanging out who, he believed, had broken into his car: "He came home one night and a group of them were standing outside his house. He went over to them and said that he didn't mind them hanging around but they weren't to throw their beer cans into his garden. One of them . . . . threatened to torch his car and his house. He decided not to call the police because he didn't want to be seen to be calling the police so he handed it over to Sinn Féin" (Student L).

The police presence can also jeopardize transactions in the informal economy. West Belfast is an area of high unemployment, and those who are employed often have low-income jobs. There is therefore a high demand for cheap goods and services. People want televisions, washing machines, and toys for their children. For some residents, survival is dependent on tolerating shady dealings: "doing the double," receiving stolen goods or doing without.[97] This informal economy depends on mutually supportive patterns of reciprocity and trust.[98] Access is thus dependent upon maintaining a reputation for being trustworthy. Contacting the police could jeopardize this reputation. First, there is a strong convention of not having anything to do with the police, and a cloud of suspicion hangs over any interaction with them. Second, any contact could unwittingly draw police attention to other illegal practices in the area. This perceived breach of trust could result in neighbors and associates becoming wary in case their operations are sabotaged, albeit unintentionally. This wariness could restrict access to affordable goods and services from the informal economy.

Finally, Dixit argues that perhaps more important than the cost advantages are the informational advantages of private arbitration and dispute resolution.[99] The rate at which offenses are cleared up by local police continues to be very low in North and West Belfast compared to other areas in Northern Ireland.[100] The lack of cooperation that the police face when investigating crimes in the area must partly explain this figure. The IRA's intimate knowledge of the community means that they are better able to gather information. In addition, they are unfettered by statutory bureaucracy and have instead adopted procedures and practices that suit their circumstances. The civil administration has a somewhat systematic approach but their rules of evidence fall short of those imposed by the Crown Prosecution Service. The result is a prompt response by the IRA. As Community Worker K remarked, "People report [to the IRA] because it's there, that's the way that it's done, and I know that it'll be dealt with fairly immediately unlike the statutory system." Not only does the IRA's access to better information mean that their response is faster, but also that they are more likely to catch the culprit. What then happens to the culprit is something that local people often prefer not to think about.

Manpower

In the chapters that follow, some of the brutality of PPAs will be conveyed. In both the academic and lay debates surrounding the informal system in West Belfast, the following question is often asked: What type of person beats and shoots young people in such a brutal manner?[101] This question asks for an answer about individual motivation, but there is also a more obvious point to be made. One reason for the existence and persistence of the system is the availability of a pool of (mostly) men, skilled in the use of violence and willing to carry out these acts as part of their duties within the IRA. The availability of manpower has been a catalyst in the business of private protection getting a foothold in other parts of the world. Gambetta argues that mafia families emerged in the United States when "the supply of and the demand for protection met: when, in other words, a sufficient number of emigrants moved there for independent reasons, some bringing along the necessary skills for organizing a protection market, and when certain events, notably the Great Depression and Prohibition, opened up a vast and lucrative market for this commodity."[102] Marina Tvetkova shows how the abundant supply of people trained in the use of violence contributed to the rise of organized crime groups in Bulgaria in the 1990s. As expected, former officers of the Ministry of the Interior, the militia, and the army were active in these groups. More unexpected was the presence of ex-athletes from the combat sports of boxing, martial arts, and, in particular, wrestling. Physically strong, trained to fight, relatively lacking in education, and facing limited employment prospects, they were ideal candidates for life as mobsters.[103]

Finding out about the perpetrators of PPAs is incredibly difficult. Victims often have criminal records and, fearing reprisals, are unwilling to make a statement to the police about the attack. Charges made against those responsible would be for the specific offenses of grievous bodily harm (GBH), actual bodily harm (ABH), and common assault. The police do not record those offenses associated with PPAs separately.[104] A search of the *Belfast Telegraph, Belfast News Letter, Irish News,* and *Irish Times* newspapers using LexisNexis news search between 1997 and 2006 resulted in fifteen cases of individuals being convicted of GBH, ABH, or common assault in association with a PPA. Of those fifteen, only Sean Patrick McGuigan was a Republican. The rest were Loyalists (see chapter 5). McGuigan was sentenced to twelve years for committing GBH. His victim suffered a fractured skull and a broken arm and leg.[105]

Alex Maskey, formerly Sinn Féin's spokesperson on policing, confirmed that IRA volunteers carry out PPAs but added that the "volunteers themselves are very critical of having to take that action. An IRA volunteer doesn't see this kind of activity as their role."[106] The suggestion that senior IRA members find the business of punishment distasteful and the job is left to "former prisoners, low calibre members and new recruits" makes intuitive sense.[107] Carrying out PPAs is a very low-risk activity in that it carries a very low probability of being convicted of any offense. Between 1994 and 1996, just one member of the IRA was convicted for every 400 attacks in the same period.[108] Once a volunteer has served a prison sentence, especially a long one, the IRA believes that individual has sacrificed enough and the volunteer will not be asked to participate in high-risk operations. New recruits, on the other hand, need to serve an apprenticeship; their level of commitment and their competence in carrying out orders must be tested, and they need to gain experience in using violence. Furthermore, carrying out a PPA compromises new recruits early in their paramilitary careers. Should they have misgivings about their involvement with the organization, their participation in illegal violence could be used as blackmail to force them to comply with the agreements they have made.[109]

During fieldwork it was suggested that "the IRA's policing role amounts to between 5 and 10 percent of the Republican Movement's total workload" (Ex-prisoner F), and PPAs are a labor-intensive activity. Of the 213 PPAs that Andrew Silke and Max Taylor studied, 56 percent were carried out by five or more individuals.[110] Both the IRA and Loyalists generally target only one person at a time, and involving this number of people seems excessive and risky. It is common, however, to involve more people than is necessary in acts of violence. If everyone is complicit, then it is in everyone's interests to stay silent lest they be implicated. A larger number of people who share the blame acts as a mechanism for cooperation and loyalty. Following the cease-fire period, the number of casualties generated by PPAs more than doubled from 86 in 1994 to 175 in 1996. As the military campaign was scaled back, either manpower was released to carry out PPAs, or there were simply more people in need of something to do.[111]

Throughout the fieldwork period, only one respondent admitted to being actively involved in the work of the civil administration and to administering a PPA. A few, like Ex-prisoner T, intimated that they had more than just a layperson's knowledge of the proceedings: "The community is making constant demands for action. It would be wrong of me to stand and do nothing about selling drugs, and I would support anyone who went out and did anything about it."

Opponents in general of the Republican Movement point to PPAs as evidence that the IRA is a group of terrorists who will callously bully and even kill their own people if necessary, but in West Belfast, opinion was mixed. Some local people were quick to condemn the IRA members who perform this policing role as thugs and criminals: "At the end of the day they are nothing more than unconvicted Schedule 1 offenders" (Youth Worker P); and hypocrites: "[T]hey're murderers who shoot the juveniles they work with during the day" (Community Worker L). Other commentators and residents were less critical. Some were keen to point out the harmful impact on those perpetrating PPAs: "Personally, I think it is very brutalising not only for the person who is having their leg broken, but my impression is that the people who do it are being brutalised as well. I'm sure that it is brutalising . . . especially going out and breaking someone's limbs" (Ex-prisoner E).

There is disagreement not just about the type of person involved but also about his motivation. Republicans argue that members of the IRA are motivated by their commitment to the local community: "I have a stake in the community and I want to see it become a better place" (Ex-prisoner T). Critics argue that those perpetrating this violence are cruel, depraved, and power driven: "[S]ome of the more sadistic elements among Loyalist and IRA members have been attracted to the job of torturing members of their own community. . . . Contrary to the impression of distaste and reluctance conveyed in paramilitary statements, the large numbers involved in beatings suggest no shortage of volunteers in search of excitement and possibly pleasure."[112]

Some respondents argued that the volunteers' motives are more complex: "I've friends who are involved in the IRA, and it's a mixture of power and service, and where the two mingle it's very hard to differentiate and separate them. In a war situation and a crisis you just react" (Community Worker S). Others commented that necessity had superseded sensibility: "It's donkey work really, and they become brutalised by the necessity of the process" (Youth Worker L).

It is certainly an oversimplification to suggest that only vicious, power-crazed thugs operate the informal system. Breidge Gadd, former Chief Probation Officer for Northern Ireland, has noted,: "These are not crazy men out of control."[113] As Burton observed, "Situations in which the IRA have used harsh and bitterly cruel methods on their own people are not hard to come by, but that is not the whole picture. The policing role of the IRA rests on their total relationship with the community, only part of which takes the guise of naked force."[114]

Residents in West Belfast fear crime: they are afraid of the destruction that joyriders and drug users and dealers bring to their streets and cul-de-sacs. This fear, combined with their reluctance to have contact with the police, has resulted in residents' reliance upon local resources. Local people often come together to act collectively and informally to control and manage the crime problem. If these collective methods do not work, and the problem of crime persists, residents will inevitably turn to the most powerful group in their midst: the IRA. Even if residents do not agree with the existence or methods of the IRA, the lack of an acceptable alternative enforcement agency has resulted in their tolerance of the IRA's punitive measures and ensured a demand for their services. The IRA has had both the motivation and the manpower to meet this demand. These measures have most often been used against persistent young offenders, known locally as hoods, and it is to this group that I will now turn to.

TWO

The Hoods

West Belfast has a high proportion of young people. According to the 2001 census, 43 percent of the population is under 24 years of age.[1] Community workers estimate that there are 2,000 young people who congregate and disperse across West Belfast's various housing developments in the evenings, which is about 7 percent of the local population.[2] They range in age from 10 to 20 years and above. Among these young people are a large number of petty offenders involved in minor delinquency. They, in turn, surround a core group of young people who persistently offend, and are known locally as *hoods*.[3]

The police estimate that between fifty and seventy hoods are responsible for the majority of crime in the West Belfast area. The composition of this core group may change over time, as some are put out of action through imprisonment or punishment, but the numbers remain fairly stable, as they are joined by new recruits. In recent years the criminological literature has focused on the issue of persistence, which is measured by a "combination of anti-social behaviour (self-reported delinquency) and contact with the police and courts (e.g., arrests and convictions)."[4] I use the term "persistent offenders" in this book to refer to those young people who have been identified by the police and the IRA as being the most frequent offenders in the West Belfast area. This chapter describes the offending and antisocial behavior that is most widespread across this group of young people, and it sets out the sanctions they receive as a result of their behavior.

Crime

Hoods share the characteristics that have been identified in many studies of persistently antisocial young people.[5] That is, they are predominantly male, begin offending early in life, have educational difficulties, suffer from a disrupted family life that involves being separated from their home, and experience poor social integration. In addition their antisocial behavior is characterized by property crimes such as car theft and burglary, as well as violence.[6]

Although the hoods are mostly male, there are also some young women whose behavior has earned them this label. In West Belfast, the roles of men and women remain strongly influenced by traditional values. For girls, being "in trouble" still carries the connotation of pregnancy rather than crime.[7] The eight young women in the sample were ages 16 to 19 years with an average age of 17, one year younger than the total group average.

These young women separate into two groups. Five of the young women dress in a masculine style and mimic the behavior of the men. They steal cars to joyride, commit burglary and theft, and take part in other forms of antisocial behavior, including drug dealing. They are verbally aggressive and have a reputation for violence. All of this group have received warnings, been placed on curfews, experienced exclusion, and received physical punishment. Lisa (age 18) was "put out of Belfast because I was joyridin'; breakin' into people's houses." Mary (age 18) claims the IRA broke both her arms but the IRA publicly stated that they had nothing to do with the attack on her.[8] Angela (age 19) was kicked and punched, covered in paint, and then beaten around the head with the paint can during a punishment attack. Julie (age 16), "got slapped by the rah [IRA]. Trailed about by the hair and got a couple of slaps and told to stay away from certain people and joyridin' and cars and stuff."

The remaining three young women form a more "ornamental" group and are more generally representative of young women in the area. They hang around with the men, but there is a limit to what offenses they will commit. Rather than risk being ridiculed if they fail at stealing and driving cars, they ride along as passengers in stolen vehicles. They also shoplift, steal, and commit frauds involving stolen or forged credit cards and false social security claims in order to support their lifestyle and their substance use. They do not have a reputation for violence, and although they may be verbally aggressive, rarely will they get involved in physical fights. The extent of the IRA's intervention with this type of young woman is often to warn them that they are "hanging around with a bad crowd," and that it would be in their best interests to find new friends and pastimes.

These findings mirror those of early studies that divided delinquent girls into two groups. In his study of gangs in 1973 in Glasgow, Scotland, James Patrick observed that female participation was either as "sexual auxiliaries or minor accomplices to the mainstream activities of male gang members,"[9] and the girls' roles have been summed up as "either tomboys or sex objects."[10] The relative invisibility of the young women and their limited participation in the riskier forms of delinquency place them beyond the scope of this study, but this is an area for further research.

None of the hoods participated in full- or part-time education. By age 14, 54 percent had been excluded from school, for violence against other pupils or teachers (38 percent), truancy (28 percent); and vandalism (15 percent). The rest simply dropped out and, once excluded, never returned to school.

Twenty-nine percent of the hoods claimed to be in some form of full-time employment. This varied in type from serving in a kebab shop to working as a painter and decorator, washing cars or performing manual labor. Their employment, however, is sporadic and they have a lot of spare time. Like average young people with time on their hands, they watch daytime television and enjoy playing or watching sports like soccer (including the Gaelic version), pool, snooker, and boxing. Their social lives extend to hanging out with their friends, clubbing, and going to pubs and the cinema.

In addition to these legitimate pursuits, the hoods characterize the rest of their lives as "runnin' about the streets and fuckin' about with my mates" (Paddy, age 19). Street life involves "hooding," that is, hanging around on street corners drinking and using drugs; fighting; stealing, shoplifting, and burglary; stealing cars and joyriding; vandalism; and selling drugs. Colin (age 17) described a typical day: "I would go out and steal somethin', sell it, get drugs, a carry out. Fly about in my mate's [stolen] car, three of us smokin' and drinkin'. Probably sit in a mate's house or go to a party—whatever comes up." To an outsider, this lifestyle appears unstructured, spontaneous, and aimless but this is what the hoods aspire to: "Drink, cars, women, drugs, money. A big long party and you don't think about reality until you sober up" (Sully, age 18). They demonstrate what has been called a "transcending commitment" to "the demands of life on the street."[11]

STREET LIFE

It is this commitment to street life that distinguishes the hoods from other young people in West Belfast. Lisa (age 18) described how she "would just be runnin' about the streets, getting' drunk, stealin' cars. Sometimes I would stay out all night and just be flyin' about in a car. I was out of the house and on the run [from the IRA] for five months." The hoods' daily preoccupations lie in when and where the next "scam" is going to take place, getting enough money for alcohol or drugs, and finding out who was "lifted" by the IRA or the police and whether that person will inform on them. Their antisocial behavior ranges from drinking on street corners to more indictable offenses (see table 1). The drugs used by the hoods were marijuana and amphetamines. None of the hoods reported using cocaine or crack.

JOYRIDING

Hoods, to a greater or lesser extent, all joyride: first stealing a car and then driving it, usually at high speed, or riding along as a passenger. Danny (age 24) said, "I was stealin' three or four cars a week, any cars really. You do the door, get in, pull the casing off, knock the ignition lock off and break the steerin' and then drive away if it starts. I'd drive it up into Poleglass until it runs out of petrol and then leave it. . . . I take them for fun."

In the past, the younger hoods would lie across the back window shelf, a practice known as "sandbagging." This was intended to act as a signal to security forces, who may have fired at a car if it was driven through a checkpoint at high speed, that they were joyriders, not paramilitaries.[12] The extra weight in the back also helps to stabilise the car as it speeds over speed bumps in the road.

Joyriders are, of course, not limited to cars, any vehicle will do. Tommy (age 23) stole a bus when he was "out with a couple of mates, high as a

Table 1
Offending and antisocial behavior among the hoods
Sample n = 72

TYPE OF OFFENSE	SELF-REPORTED (1999)		ACTUAL CONVICTIONS (1999)	
	Number of hoods	*% of sample*	*Number of hoods*	*% of sample*
Joyriding related offense	60	83	9	13
Violence against the person	65	90	5	7
Robbery	10	14	0	0
Burglary	25	35	3	4
Theft	58	81	6	8
Substance abuse	72	100	0	0
Drug dealing	7	10	0	0
Other offenses	34	47	2	3

Source: Author's compilation. The names and dates of birth of the hoods in the sample were given to the Northern Ireland Office Statistics and Research Agency, which provided anonymized data on actual convictions. These data were then reconstructed under the broader categories listed.

kite." He eventually drove the bus off the road and abandoned it to be set on fire by some up-and-coming younger hoods.

Joyriders will commonly steal cars from other areas of Belfast and then drive them into West Belfast. However, they need to choose their target areas carefully. In 1998, the Ulster Defence Association (UDA), a Loyalist paramilitary group in the Shankill (the Protestant area that borders Catholic West Belfast), issued a warning to Catholic young people: "We don't tolerate this sort of thing from the hoods in our community and we are not going to tolerate it from people outside the area."[13] This was reiterated by a spokesman for the Ulster Democratic Party (UDP), the political representatives of the UDA, when he stated, "I am very concerned about what will happen if people get their hands on them. . . . I think there will be a risk to their lives."[14] On this occasion the warning appeared to take effect and the hoods retreated behind the sectarian boundary. Their recklessness within their local areas, however, continued unabated.

Joyriding is the hoods' showpiece activity. It is highly visible and very risky. Nearly every night, and particularly during the summer months, from approximately eleven o'clock onward, joyriders are on the streets of West Belfast. The adult residents of the various developments watch in anger while the younger children look on with a mixture of envy and admiration. Liam (age 21) lives in one such development and grew up with many of the hoods. He observed the excitement that the joyriders generate: "I would've been tempted. I'd come out of the house to watch all of those stolen cars being driven by lots of my friends and people I knew. I'd cheer them on, hand brakin' and everything and all the other kids would be goin' mad shoutin' and cheerin' at them."

When asked why they drove stolen cars, all of the joyriders talked about "the buzz"—the excitement and rush of adrenaline that accompanies driving a stolen car at high speed and provides a respite from the boredom of everyday life: "Only when I'm bored do I go out, which is often. I'm not makin' any money out of it, it's just for fun" (Micky, age 18). For some hoods, simply being in a stolen car provides enough thrill: "I haven't stolen them myself but I get in stolen cars. . . . My mates would stop and say do you want to go for a wee spin and I'd get in and get a buzz out of it" (Tim, age 17). Other hoods prefer both to steal and drive the cars themselves: "I was stealing cars about once a week or something. I was stealin' them just to joyride on my own. I was doin' it for fun because there was nothin' to do in Belfast" (Gerry, age 22). All of the joyriders interviewed use drugs and alcohol to intensify the buzz. Tim (age 17), gets into a stolen car "instead of standin' at a street corner getting frozen plus I'd have a few swallows [drinks] in me, gettin' hyper. I'd usually have been drinkin' before I get in a car." This causes the police additional problems: "[T]he vast majority who we [the police] catch and bring in for interview aren't deemed fit for interview because they are high on drugs, glue or drink" (Member of the PSNI Driving Away Team).

Joyriders exaggerate the risks they take by playing "chicken games" or trying to race police vehicles and taxis. They look for cruising police patrol vehicles and try to provoke a high-speed chase. Alex (age 19) was hospitalized following one of these chases: "The police rammed us into a wall and my cheek got sliced right through." The police also reported instances of joyriders repeatedly ramming police vehicles. In the past, when security checkpoints were more common, joyriders would accelerate through police and army barriers inviting gunfire, sometimes with fatal consequences.[15]

The joyriders also target taxi drivers: "The game they play is to drive at high speed and then brake as they knock into them to try and scare the taxi driver."[16] I interviewed ten taxi drivers about the problems they faced. Ken was chased out of a West Belfast development by two cars driven by joyriders: "My heart was in my mouth but I swore I would never ever go back up into that estate again," he said. Jim described being rammed by joyriders: "Well if they hit you like and they're going the speed they're going at. . . . It mightn't be so bad if they hit you frontal but if they hit you side on, you know, there's nothing there for protection." He claimed joyriders regularly tried to provoke him into driving dangerously:

> Joyriders seem to have the tendency of trying to race me and I've no intentions of trying to race them—you don't want to know you just don't want to fucking have anything to do with them. But I've seen them on a Saturday night and me going up the Monagh by-pass and they're behind me and they're flashing and they're beeping and they're trying to get you to go that wee bit faster and race them.

Simply plying their trade in West Belfast jeopardizes the lives of taxi drivers and their passengers, for whom encountering a joyrider is a terrifying experience. As Gerry, a driver who works exclusively in West Belfast, pointed out, "They don't care, and my taxi's my livelihood."[17]

Lack of control and recklessness increases with intoxication and with cars being driven at 100 mph, accidents are all too common.[18] Davy (age 17) had been in three nearly fatal incidents: "Half the time I don't even remember whether I've been driving a car or not" he said. Angela (age 19) was in a lot of pain after injuring her back. She had been a passenger in a stolen car, driven by a female friend, when it crashed following a chase by the police. Tony (age 24) claimed he had been shot and injured by the British army when he crashed through a security checkpoint. Tragically, some hoods do not survive. Twelve months after being interviewed for this study, 20-year-old Brian Donnelly was a passenger in a stolen Vauxhall Cavalier. Traveling at 100 mph, the car ploughed into another car containing a young couple and two young children. Brian and the two adults in the other vehicle were killed.

As with young men generally, the type and make of car that a joyrider drives has implications for his reputation and social status. Some therefore preferred the challenge and kudos of larger, more powerful, and expensive cars. Sammy (age 18) boasted that he had "the best cars on the estate" and Dessie (age 18) specialized in four-wheel-drives: "I steal a car for money. I would sell pieces of the car or the whole car for money—it just depends." Some joyriders will also exchange cars for drugs, either for their personal use or to sell on and make a profit.

Driving at high speed, doing hand-brake turns, ramming into houses, vehicles, and lampposts, and ram-raiding shop windows are the staple diet of a night of joyriding. A small number of hoods develop more sophisticated and profitable operations stealing cars or car parts to sell, sometimes to fulfill orders. Some also become middlemen, getting younger thieves to steal for them. The cars are then passed through a network of cutting shops and "ringer factories." The majority of hoods are joyriders, but they are also involved with other types of antisocial behavior.

ONE-ON-ONE VIOLENCE

Black eyes, as well as cuts and bruises to their bodies and faces, are common among the hoods. Some of these injuries come from car accidents, but many result from interpersonal violence: "I get into fights nearly every weekend for nothing. I just seem to come out of the pub and get in a fight" (Brendan, age 17). Twenty-nine percent of the sample had been arrested and charged with assault in the six-month period prior to the fieldwork, but they all reported frequent involvement in violent incidents. Angela (age 19) was the only hood who was subsequently convicted of an assault charge.

Local residents fear that the hoods' verbal aggression will escalate to a violent assault, and there have been many cases of intimidation and attacks on property.[19] Generally, though, the hoods' violence is directed against other hoods, and is often fuelled by alcohol. Verbal aggression can quickly escalate into physical violence: "When I get mad I start to slabber [make violent threats] like fuck. . . . I gave this wee fella a hidin' the other week. He was a vicious wee cunt that's all I can remember 'cause I'd been drinkin' for a while (Micky, age 18).

In most situations the fight will be a fistfight or involve a blunt instrument. As Micky explained, "[Y]ou have to know how to swing a snooker cue around here." Knife attacks are increasingly common. Danny (age 24), who had slashed someone across the face with a knife after a fight had broken out, also told me, "My girl's ex-boy [boyfriend] came to the door and he was slabberin' at her for ages. Anyway we saw him later that week and I stuck a knife in him. He won't come near my door again in a hurry." Danny also admitted to slashing someone across the face with a knife after a fight broke out.

Not only are hoods the chief perpetrators of violence, but they are often victims as well.[20] Dermot (age 17) got hit on the head with a brick during a fight, and Alex (age 18) described how he got set upon, paramilitary style, by a group of other hoods:

> I got beat up with hurley bats for personal reasons. I'm not saying who it was, but it was nothing to do with a punishment beating. I was supposed to have said that I was gonna stab him [one of the attackers] and then him and his mates came up to Turf [Lodge] and hit me with hurley bats and I woke up a day later in hospital.

Violence is also directed against property. Schools, youth clubs, and playgroups have been broken into and wrecked by, in most cases, younger hoods intent on doing as much damage as possible. Other aspects of the hoods' violence will be explored in chapter 4.

BURGLARY, ROBBERY, AND THEFT

Hoods' employment is sporadic, they have little money and will steal goods to sell in order to buy clothes, alcohol, and drugs. Younger hoods and young women favor petty shoplifting from high-end stores in Belfast city center: "If you want money you just go downtown and get it—just go down and snatch somethin'" (Máire, age 16). I witnessed Colin (age 17) being seized by security guards in a city-center shopping arcade after CCTV cameras had filmed him stuffing clothes underneath his jacket.

He grew up in a family of "fences" (specialists in selling stolen goods), and his father had served several prison sentences for theft and receiving stolen goods: "My dad has been in prison before for lots of different things. He's been goin' to prison since I was a baby. . . . I'm stealing a few pairs of jeans, sellin' 'em, and then bein' skint. I go into town, do it, and then sell it to anyone that wants." Sully (age 18) went snatching because he enjoyed the thrill of getting away with it: "I steal a few things—snatches with clothes, wear them myself or else sell them on— I love making money for nothing."

Older hoods have ram-raided jewelry shops, and have committed burglary and armed robbery. The lure of seemingly easy money is strong, but the risks can be very high. Psycho (age 20) was kneecapped for his role in the burglary of the home of an IRA member: "I'm not going to stop offending, I don't want to stop—there's too much money to be made. I steal cars, ram-raid and am basically into everything."

Invariably, the hoods spend a substantial amount of the money made in this way on drugs and alcohol.

Substance Abuse

All of the hoods use drugs and alcohol and generally begin their substance abuse with solvents at the age of just 10 or 11. Solvents hold a strong attraction: they are cheap and accessible, and have powerful effects. Glue was once the main substance for inhalation in West Belfast, but correction fluids and thinners, butane gas in aerosols, gas lighter refills, and gas cylinders are all used extensively. Hoods gather in graveyards, in empty lots, and on street corners to drink, sniff solvents, or smoke marijuana:

> I smoke blow [marijuana] everyday. I make somethin' to eat and have some blow. After I eat, I phone my mates to ask if they're goin' out, go into town with them, if I've the money I would smoke blow again. We'd probably have four grams between three or four of us if we drink that would do us, if not, go out and get more. If I'd the money I'd buy it, if not steal it, mostly every day it happens. I like getting stoned, the hit of it, it's just a daily thing like smoking fags. You'd be tired but your behaviour doesn't change. I would go stealing but it [drugs]

doesn't make me do it. I have ten friends who smoke, same as me, same boat, we do it together. (Colin, age 17)

Sully (age 18) has "taken just about every single drug there is to take—Es, blow, acid, speed, but I don't take them all on a regular basis. I smoke one or two joints a day and then acid and speed mainly at the weekends when you can get hold of it. I take alcohol every day – case of beer, a couple of bottles of cider . . ." Angela (age 19), who had a cleaning job, said it helped her get her work done as she would " just fly around with the Hoover" after taking ecstasy.

There is an expectation among the hoods that their substance abuse will change over time and they will move off solvents and on to alcohol, marijuana, ecstasy, and other drugs: "They [solvents] can lead to some-thin' else, especially when you're young—you like the hit and want to try somethin' else" (Colin, age 17). Those who continue to use glue past the age of the 15 or 16 are looked down upon. Furthermore, they were aware of just how damaging solvent abuse was. Gerry (age 22) had a daily habit of sniffing about one litre of glue every day:

> There's a good buzz off it, but it kills your brain cells and ruins your liver and you always get into trouble with it 'cause you don't know what you're doin'. It can make you do all the things that you don't want to do like stealin' an' stuff. My mate hung himself and died, God rest his soul, and that's another reason I want to go off it 'cause I don't want to end up like him. I want to stay off it permanently.

Addiction may be both physiological and psychological: taking illicit substances is thrilling and can lead to further offending. The link between using drugs and alcohol and joyriding is very strong. Danny (age 24) told me, "If I didn't take drugs I wouldn't steal cars, and I have to take drugs to have a good time. I take Es and blow. I take Es every weekend and lose count after the second." When I interviewed Sully (age 18) in the Young Offenders Institute (YOI), he said, "I'm always at it, as soon as I get out of here [Hydebank Young Offenders Center (YOC)] I'll be blocked [drunk]. I was drunk on Friday and in cars, got in a car on Saturday and got caught on Sunday—I wouldn't have been in the car if I was sober." Depression, however, may follow: "I'm smoking four or five joints every couple of days. I want to stop because it does your head in. I just want to stop taking drugs. It eats into your money. It makes you feel good, mellow out now and again and go asleep. I feel a bit depressed sometimes when I wake up," said Colm (age 17). Tim (age 17) agreed: "The cost is the next day—I'm fucked. Feelin' sick, can't eat, teeth are like raw. It also costs me money because I can't work and fuckin' the rest of the day up for yerself." Máire (age 16) was taking so many ecstasy tablets that Angela described her as "rattlin' when she walks":

> It's hard, everything's hard. It's hard tryin' to stop but I can't stop. I'm usin' all the time; smokin' blow nearly every night of the week and takin' Es every weekend. I would like to be clean and normal like other wee girls do at my age—go to school, go to work, do a bit of housework, havin' a family night in, goin' out at the weekend, but then I think, what's the point? I do and I don't, when I'm down I do, when I'm up I don't. (Máire, age 16)

The hoods also spoke about a number of their friends who had died as a result of drug-related suicides. Although she was drug dealing at the time, Angela (age 19) said, "Drugs put everybody's head away and it's worse when you come off them—two of my friends came off drugs for a while and then they both killed themselves."

A similar pattern of responses emerged about alcohol: "The effect of drink is dependent on the company you're in. The only thing that you can be sure of is that it'll change your mood," said Sean (age 17).[21] Dessie (age 18) believes that he would be a more successful car thief if he didn't drink so much: "My life is bad. I drink too much and then I steal cars. I would rather steal cars when I'm not drinkin' 'cause I would make more money. I wouldn't crash so many." Whereas Mary (age 18) recognized that drinking was a symptom as well as a cause of her unhappiness, "I'm not happy at the minute. I drink every night, it's causin' me problems. I'd like to be just a social drinker."

Nevertheless, for most of the hoods living with the negative consequences of using solvents, drugs, and alcohol is better than the boredom and frustration that accompanies not using these substances: "I get pissed off and I start sniffing again. I sniff when I get bored" (Bobby, age 20). Jackie (age 17) agreed: "When you come off the drugs there is nothing to do and nowhere to go."

Drug Dealing

It proved to be very difficult to collect data on drug dealing in West Belfast. The hoods were very reluctant to talk about where their drugs came from and it was difficult to get any real sense of the extent of drug dealing among the group. However, the evidence from those hoods who did admit to selling drugs suggests that they were dealing on a small scale. Angela (age 19) provides a typical example of the extent of the dealing. When first asked where she got her drugs from, she replied, "I don't pay for mine, I get mine for nothing." It then transpired that two of her uncles operated a sizeable drug-dealing business, and prior to their deaths (they were both executed by the IRA), they would give her drugs, which she either kept or sold to her friends. Following the murders of her uncles, she continued to sell, albeit on a small scale. Despite being all too aware of the risks she was running, she remained relatively blasé about it: "I was bored and pissed off and had no money, so that's why I started. What some people would earn in a week, I'd earn in a day."

Micky (age 18) was the one exception to this pattern of small-scale dealing. The IRA had excluded him five consecutive times from Northern Ireland for selling drugs. Micky would leave the country when ordered, but would start dealing again upon his return. He claimed that his business was very profitable: "I was selling [drugs] over the summer. I always seem to end up selling them, Es and blow, about two hundred and fifty Es a week, every week. I have a couple of sources."

Hoods like Micky found the easy money from drug dealing very tempting despite the likelihood of being punished: "I think I might have seen the light about dealing. I know I'll get shot next time unless I can get away with it on the fly. The trouble with stoppin' is that you always end up skint and then you are tempted. That's what it's all about—money."

Punishment

The hood's offending is so visible and frequent that it is not long before they come face to face with the authorities. "Bringing trouble to the

Table 2
Formal and informal punishments received by the hoods
n=72

TYPE OF PUNISHMENT (FORMAL)	NUMBER OF HOODS	% OF SAMPLE
Community sentence	43	60
Detention in a secure unit or a YOI*	45	63

TYPE OF PUNISHMENT (INFORMAL)	NUMBER OF HOODS	% OF SAMPLE
Warning	70	97
Curfew	54	75
Exclusion/exile	32	44
Beating	29	40
Shooting	5	7

*Youth Offenders Institute

Source: Author's compilation. In order to get information about formal sentencing, the names and dates of birth of the hoods in the sample were given to the Northern Ireland Office Statistics and Research Agency, who provided anonymized data on actual sentences. These data were then reconstructed under the broader categories listed.

door" can mean either a visit from the police, and subsequent processing though the criminal justice system, or from the IRA. Table 2 sets out the different types of punishments that the hoods in the sample received between 1998 and 2002.

In addition, many of the hoods have been punished by both systems—the police and the IRA. Twenty-two (31 percent) had both been in detention and been a victim of a PPA. That is, they had received severe punishments from both systems.

FORMAL

The difficulties in policing West Belfast have been well documented but nonetheless, hoods do get caught, convicted, and sentenced by the criminal justice system. Many of the sample were well known to the police and especially to the units established to combat joyriding.[22] In 1998, forty-five (63 percent) reported having spent time in some form of detention, in either a secure unit or a YOI, and during 1999, forty-one (57 percent) of the sample were convicted at court in Northern Ireland (see table 2).[23] It is generally accepted that there is a degree of antipathy between local people in this area and the criminal justice agencies, but the hoods' hostility toward the police seems to have more to do with attempts to thwart their offending than with any political differences.

Hoods portray an elaborate game of "can't catch me" or "hide and seek" with the police. Declan (age 17) described how he would regularly hide in a cupboard when the police came searching for him. Sammy (age 18) claimed that he could always "outsmart the cops," and the hoods often appeared fairly successful at out-maneuvering the police, but this may in part be due to the police's limited ability to police effectively in West Belfast rather than the hoods' wiliness.

Davy (age 17) and his friends got involved in what became reported in the local press as a "siege" with the police. According to Davy, he and his brothers ran out of alcohol during a party, and so they robbed the local liquor store. The police traced the theft to the partying hoods, who met them with a tirade of abuse while hanging out of a second-floor window wielding hurley sticks, aiming a large water pistol, and throwing beer bottles and cans. The police donned riot gear and stormed the house. The whole face-off lasted several hours and was reported in the *Belfast Telegraph* with the headline of "Police storm siege drama house— Nine arrested after stand-off."[24]

Tony (age 24) described how he and his friends would regularly ambush police and army patrols by jeering and then throwing beer cans at them. A beer can, although relatively harmless, could easily be mistaken for a petrol bomb in an area notorious for paramilitary ambushes.

For the hoods, the threat of being placed in some sort of detention by the police concerned them less than the hassle of being stopped and searched regularly: "When the cops all get to know you, you get stopped everywhere you go," said Micky (age 18). Other hoods were also bothered by having a criminal record: "The trouble is your charge sheet if you get caught: you'll never get a job because of your criminal record," commented Paul (age 16).

Their relative disregard for the criminal justice system was evidenced in the way they would forget to attend court hearings, and if they did attend, their manner was invariably sullen and disrespectful. Community sentences were ignored or adhered to selectively. According to Danny (age 24), "On probation they send you on a course and you don't know what the fuck is goin' on or what is happenin'. I wouldn't do a probation order—I always got breached." Sixty percent had received the more severe sentence of time in a secure unit or a YOI, and they talked about this experience cavalierly. Sammy (age 18) viewed the YOI he was in as "a gift"—an opportunity to "get his head together" and take some time out from his chaotic life on the streets. This view was generally expressed among the hoods who also enjoyed the marijuana they could get inside prison: "You can get anything in Hydebank. I smoke blow every single day and night in Hydebank. It puts me to sleep, calms me down, otherwise, I would crack up in here all day. I keep comin' into Hydebank to get dried out and then go back out again" (Sully, age 18).

Some of the older hoods expressed concern about the prospect of an adult prison. In Northern Ireland, where the minimum age for sentencing to an adult prison is twenty-one, this possibility seemed remote, however, for many of the younger hoods.

INFORMAL

Of much greater concern to all the hoods was the possibility of facing the informal system of policing and punishment in West Belfast. The IRA administers this informal system, and all of the hoods in this study had fallen foul of it, in some way (see table 2).

The informal system in West Belfast is characterized by a proportional tariff of punishments, some of which are very violent. Over the past thirty years Sinn Féin and the IRA have developed guidelines dictating who should be punished, why they should be punished, and how they should be punished. Everyone who is involved appears to understand the vagaries of the system, particularly which actions and individuals "deserve" punishment, and what those punishments should be. Specific decisions may be hotly debated, but everyone grasps the broad framework and apparatus:

There is a line that is drawn. It's hard to say where exactly that line is. How many times someone is caught joyridin' or nickin' stuff. But everyone just knows when enough is enough. If someone is being a real menace, and the community keep reporting him, then the IRA will investigate and come up with a lot of stuff, or this person is known to us then they will have to act. Everybody knows what has to be done, and they [sic] know what's coming to them. (Ex-prisoner C)

The IRA bases its judgments on the crime, the circumstances surrounding the crime, and the background of the offender. This is illustrated by the following extract from an information leaflet issued by the Republican movement justifying their punishment of John Toal and Brian Hamill, who were both involved in antisocial behavior. Toal also confessed to being a police informant:

Belfast Brigade IRA claims responsibility for the punishment beating in Beechmount on Thursday night of Brian Hamill, who lives with his grandmother in West Street. Along with John Toal and others, Hamill was involved not only in persistent 'joyriding' but in repeated burglaries of shops in the Beechmount area. Five or six shops were robbed by this gang in a single night on at least three separate occasions last month alone. Hamill, who has been warned by us several times, was tarred and feathered by the IRA a month ago, but ignored this punishment. Therefore, in addition to Thursday's punishment we have no option, in view of the lack of control exercised by his grandmother Anne, who condoned his activities, but to warn Hamill to stay out of the Falls area in future. We also take this opportunity to warn local people against buying property which they know or suspect to be stolen.

Six other people involved in this gang have again been spoken to by the Republican movement, and warned about their activities. They have been told to stay in their own homes each night after 9 pm [curfew].

Having reviewed John Toal's age, and the fact that he came forward without prompting to confess his RUC informer activities, we have decided not to physically punish him despite the extreme seriousness of what he has done. However, both for his own protection from futher RUC approaches, and particularly for the protection of the community, Toal has been informed that he must now leave the country [exiling] within 48 hours.[25]

These judgments are not always so transparent and are perhaps clearer to "insiders" than to outside observers, who do not understand the mitigating or aggravating circumstances in specific cases. While the IRA may argue that ideally their judgments are value-led and proportional, it often appears that their dispensation of punishments is not ideological, but dictated by circumstances and resources:

> [T]he Republican movement had a very limited set of tariffs or sanctions they could impose on crimes. . . . If a person had been accused of joyriding, he would be shot, by the same token, if a person was accused of sexual abuse he would also be shot so there was very little distinction. Again, it was because of the limited resources that the IRA had . . . they couldn't put people in jail, they couldn't give them community service, they couldn't put them on probation, so they had a very different set of options that they could work with. The two main ones were either exclusion or physical punishment. (Ex-prisoner E).

The IRA's decisions may be contested but they insist that, within their social and political constraints, their system is proportional and as fair as it can be. The hoods received the following types of punishment.

Warning
As a first intervention, the IRA may issue a simple warning and for many this is enough to deter future antisocial behavior. Lorraine, a social worker, described how as a teenager she and her sister began drinking on the street with a group of known hoods. It was not long before the IRA visited her home and warned them to stop immediately. The combination of the IRA's visit and the resulting wrath of her father frightened her so much that for about six months afterward she refused to leave her house in the evenings in case her presence on the street was interpreted as defiance rather than simply a visit to the corner shop. Joe Austin, a Sinn Féin councillor, reported to Human Rights Watch that

> if a 17-year-old is accused of housebreaking—breaking and entering—and there's proof of it, the parents will be visited by the IRA.

They'll give evidence to the parents and advise the parents that their son is involved with bad company, or is drinking, or is a substance abuser, and tell parents that they should keep an eye on the boy. If there is a second incident with the boy, the IRA will visit the parents again, and the boy will be curfewed—he might have to be home by ten o'clock every night for about three months.[26]

A Sinn Féin youth worker confirmed this:

These beatings don't come out of nowhere. People live in close communities and parents will themselves ask for some sort of intervention from Sinn Féin—something to give people a short, sharp shock. Simply just to scare their child a bit. So, someone will come round and have a word with them and so it continues. There is a process of protracted negotiation and mediation. (Sinn Féin Youth Worker H)

Warnings are commonly given privately and some hoods even claimed that they have received messages while in detention that they would be punished when they were released. Sully (age 18), who was in a YOC, said he was expecting to hear any day that he was threatened: "I don't know if I'm under threat or not yet 'cause one of the wee girls caught with me, her da's in doin' time for the rah. I don't really give a fuck either 'cause they'll not be able to get me in here and when I get out I'm buggering off to Holland. So as for the rah, fuck 'em!" Public warnings are also issued with lists posted on walls naming people who are under threat.

Curfew

If a warning has not been heeded or the offense is more serious, a curfew is imposed. Joe Austin said, "If there is a second incident with the boy, the IRA will visit the parents again, and the boy will be curfewed; he might have to be home by 10 pm every night for about three months."[27] The curfew is often enforced with parental support, but the IRA will make spot-checks to ensure compliance. It is impossible to give any figures of the number of young people who have been warned or placed on a curfew. No one ever formerly reports being on a curfew, and, consequently, no individual or agency records cases. However, 35 percent of the hoods admitted to having been placed on a curfew, and 13 percent claimed they were on a curfew when I interviewed them.

Danny, Mark, Micky and Georgie carelessly left a window open while they were smoking marijuana and talking about drugs. Their conversation was overheard by a couple of IRA members who were outside the window: "[T]hey were standin' outside the house listenin' to us talkin' about drugs. They strip-searched us, kicked us about the living room, made us lie face down on the kitchen floor with the lights out. I thought I was gettin' my legs broke," reported Danny (age 24). Initially, the four hoods were given forty-eight hours to leave the country, but after some mediation on their behalf by a local priest, their punishment was reduced to a three-month curfew. Although this was a more lenient punishment, the four objected bitterly to the restriction on their movements and the resulting boredom: "You can't really do much on an eight o'clock curfew other than smoke blow, watch football, that's it," said Georgie (age 21). Micky (age 18) added, "I'm on an eight o'clock curfew. I'm not allowed to run about with my friends. What am I supposed to do all night?" Despite the circumstances in which they were apprehended, Danny (age 24) still protested his innocence: "Being curfewed is doin' my head in—bein' treated like a child for somethin' I didn't do. I don't get to see my mates. I'm not allowed to see them after eight o'clock. If we're seen together, we'll be put out. I wanna be able to walk about free and not have to look over my shoulder."

If the hoods get caught breaking their curfew, then the punishment increases in severity: "I was attacked when I broke my curfew and they tried to break my legs. Now I'm excluded for burnin' a stolen car on Poleglass," said Tom (age 19).

Exclusion or Exiling

Exclusion can take a number of increasingly extensive forms ranging from local banishment to being excluded from the country. Although they do collaborate, the IRA's policing units often make autonomous decisions, and it is therefore possible for an excluded person to move from one Republican area to another.[28] Even if the units communicate with one another, they differ in their ability to enforce decisions, as one respondent noted: "The level of control that the paramilitaries have depends on what area of West Belfast you live in and what streets within that area. Inner Beechmount, Ballymurphy, Lower Falls, Turf Lodge are more highly controlled" (Ex-prisoner P). Often, offenders will not come to any physical harm, providing that they do not acquire a profile similar to the one they had in the area from which they were excluded (Conway 1994: 119). If a hood has to leave West Belfast only, he will be given twenty-four hours to get out or face a more severe physical punishment. Those who are ordered out of the country are given a longer deadline in recognition of their need to get "things sorted," such as finding somewhere to go and getting the wherewithal to leave. Georgie (age 21) who has been "put out of the country three times in three years," was given forty-eight hours to leave for Manchester.

A variable time limit is placed on exclusions. It can range from weeks, through months, or years, to a permanent exclusion in the most serious cases. Family members can attempt to negotiate the removal of an exclusion order or a reduction in the time involved, with promises of lessons having been learned and predictions of future good behavior. Gerard Groogan (age 18) and his brother Michael (age 16) were excluded from Ireland for antisocial behavior. After some negotiation on their behalf, they were both permitted to return to Northern Ireland for their father's funeral. Gerard, however, was ordered to leave immediately after the funeral was over.[29] Once excluded, returning to an area without permission will result in additional penalties. Depending on the original reasons for exile, the extra punishment could be extended time away or a violent punishment attack.

Most hoods prefer exile to places where they have some form of existing social network such as family or friends who will accommodate them on short notice. Sammy (age 18), who has been excluded from Belfast numerous times, said, "I've been put out of the country four times for four to five months at a time. I go to Portaferry to my aunt's house. My uncle got me back in again and I stayed out of trouble for a week and then got back into it again." However, if such support does not exist, they may choose exile in either the Republic of Ireland or one of the larger cities in England, such as London, Manchester, or Liverpool.

Exclusion is rarely a positive experience for hoods. Many have underdeveloped personal and social skills and are unable to access networks of support that would enable them to survive.[30] Danny (age 24) was adamant that he was not going back to Dublin or England, because "there are too many drugs and I'd have just ended up a bigger junkie, what's the point of that?" He described how his behavior deteriorated as a result of being homeless and having to live in a hostel: "Puttin' me out my own area only made me worse. I was less likely to do stuff in my own area. But, see livin' away and sleepin' in hostels and stuff, it just does your head in and you go mad."

Faced with the loneliness and isolation of life elsewhere, some hoods prefer to take their chances and remain in West Belfast. Despite being excluded for joyriding Davy (age 17) was determined to stay and risk being shot: "The IRA'll never keep me out of Turf Lodge, and the only way they'll be able to do that is if they put a bullet in my head and carry me out in a box." He was insistent that he had the right to "walk about as he pleased" and, as we shall see, being the victim of a particularly brutal punishment beating made him more defiant.

Other hoods leave, but return for a variety of reasons before their exclusion is over. Paul McDonald was expelled from Ireland because of his antisocial behavior. He defied this exclusion and returned to Northern Ireland for the birth of his baby. Following his return, Paul was attacked in his home, beaten with baseball bats and a hammer and then shot in the right elbow, both thighs and his right leg. He also suffered a fractured skull and multiple bruising.[31]

Beatings

Punishment beatings are not all the same.[32] Some of the beatings are not much more than a "cuff around the ear," and some victims, like Julie (age 16), are quite cavalier about it: "The rah used to torture me. I got slapped by the rah. Trailed about by the head and got a couple of slaps and told to stay away from certain people and joyriding and cars and stuff." Other punishments are much more severe and require lengthy periods of hospitalization: "I was beaten twice, once with hurley bats and once with golf clubs for antisocial behavior. I was hospitalised when I got the blame for breakin' a window in Turf Lodge," said Steve (age 18). Owen (age 25) reported that he'd been "baseball batted and sledge hammered, and I've had a few tickin' offs as well from the paramilitaries for burglary and car theft. I was put in hospital after a punishment beating, I was beaten on the legs, the hands, and the back with a baseball bat and a sledge hammer."

The most common IRA practice is to beat someone with baseball bats, hurley sticks, or cudgels, which are often spiked with nails. The force of the beating can cause the nails to split the flesh, resulting in very nasty large open puncture wounds. Iron bars and any instrument with the capacity of causing serious injury to limbs are also used. Michael had concrete slabs dropped on his limbs, breaking both his legs and arms. Michael's legs had been broken once before during a PPA when he was beaten with a fire extinguisher.

Angela was 17 years old when she was abducted, blindfolded, and taken to the backyard of a terraced house. Angela alleges she was attacked by members of Cumann na mBan,[33] the IRA's female unit, who poured a can of paint over her and then beat her about the head with the paint can. Angela was also punched in the face several times. Angela believes that the IRA had deliberately selected Cumann na mBan from outside her local area, so she would be unable to recognize any of them.

Angela's offense was drug dealing, an enterprise she got involved with because she said it was "so easy." Her dealing was on a very small scale. Two of her uncles ran sizeable drug dealing operations, and, in a sense, it was a family business. After obtaining her supply from one of her uncles, she would sell locally to friends, primarily to fund her own drug and alcohol habit and to enable her to buy clothes (although most of the time she would simply steal these). The IRA had warned Angela repeatedly, and she expected an attack at any time. She believed that her sentence was relatively lenient, however, because her estranged father had powerful "connections" with the IRA, and had protected her for as long has he could.

The sentence imposed on Angela's uncles (her mother's brothers) was not so lenient. A notice was posted in a variety of bars and public places in the Lower Falls area of West Belfast. At the top of the notice was written the following:

THESE PEOPLE DAMAGE YOUR CHILDREN
IF YOU SEE ANY OF THEM RING THIS NUMBER.

Beneath these words was a list of twelve names that over time were ticked off one by one as the persons named were shot dead. There is now a tick beside Angela's uncles' names, and she continues to wear an engraved medallion of one of her dead uncles.

Davy, who had been excluded for joyriding and had gained some notoriety from participating in the "siege," had also been the victim of a horrific beating. Twelve months before being interviewed, the IRA had kidnapped him, covered his eyes with tape, and bound his hands behind his back. Then, they hung him upside-down from railings and beat him repeatedly with baseball bats embedded with nails until his legs were broken. Davy hung on the railings, unable to get down and in agony, until a by-passer rescued him and phoned for an ambulance. He subsequently spent three weeks in the hospital and several months recovering. He claims he was falsely accused of the ram-raid of a shop belonging to a Republican family, which led to the IRA's intimidation of his family and his punishment. He insists that he could not have been responsible because he was in a YOC at the time the robbery took place. Nonetheless, the IRA had gone to his home on a number of occasions before the attack, where they had held his parents hostage in the hope that he would return home while they were there. Finally, when one of Davy's friends arrived at the house the IRA kidnapped him, bundled him into a car, and then, with a gun to his head, made him direct them to the places he might expect to find Davy. Although the IRA did not apologize to Davy in person, he claims they told his father that, on this occasion, they had punished the wrong person.

Shooting
Since the 1970s the IRA have relied heavily on various forms of shooting to keep their communities in order. The most notorious is kneecapping: "The shootings are a clear stamp of IRA authority. . . . It was always a mark of the IRA that people got shot in the kneecaps." (Ex-prisoner E). For the IRA, this trademark "is a way of punishment and incapacitation, a physical indication that something has been done, a bit like prison—it is a very visible sign of punishment" (Ex-prisoner F). The basic form of kneecapping is where the victim is forced to lie face down on the ground and is shot in the back of the knees. Once the IRA decides to kneecap someone, the punishment may still vary by the number of limbs shot, the calibre of the weapon used, and the position of the wound relative to the

joint.[34] A bullet through the fleshy part of the thigh is a light sentence; a heavy sentence could destroy arteries and bones.[35] Thus, the severity of the shooting relates to the severity of the offense.

Some people interviewed had been shot three or four times, healed, and were out again offending, and so the IRA tried to do greater damage. They shot them through the back of the knee, in the popliteal artery. If untreated, there is reduced blood flow, and this can cause amputations.[36]

The IRA maintains that if the person handling the gun knows what he is doing, the injury is usually not too severe. A victim is often able to walk normally again after about three weeks of convalescence.[37]

Further variations of shooting include the "Padre Pio," where victims are shot through both hands;[38] a "six-pack," where a shot is fired into each knee, ankle and thigh—six bullets in total; a "fifty-fifty" is so-called because a shot is fired into the base of the victim's spine, leaving them with a 50 percent chance of permanent paralysis from the waist down; and finally, there is execution.

Many of the hoods will be on the run for some time, moving from house to house, going out only after dark and staying away from regular stamping grounds before the IRA will catch up with them. Kenny (age 17) told me, "I never really see my ma. I just run in and out of the house, no time to talk to her 'cause I can't stay there." Their vigilance—as described by a former hood, Gary (age 17), who was "always looking over my shoulder, having to keep the car doors locked"—is warranted. In April 2000, a number of masked Republicans surrounded a car on the Turf Lodge housing development and began smashing the windows with clubs. The driver of the car managed to get away, but the 19-year-old passenger was dragged from the vehicle and shot in both legs. The report in the local newspaper stated that the driver of the car had disappeared.[39]

Constantly having to be on guard can take its toll on the hoods, who use alcohol and drugs to relax: "I was worried about getting grabbed by someone . . . every time I heard a car pull up I'd be looking out all the while. That made me drink more," said Gary (age 17), recalling his former days as a hood. Gary's sister Mary (age 18) had her arms broken in a punishment beating: "I can't go over the door—the rah are after me. I'm not happy at the minute and I drink every night." However, West Belfast is a small place and eventually the IRA will catch up with them. Sammy (age 18) was first caught in a fish and chip shop:

> I was in the chippy, slabberin' away, and these two rah men came in. They chased me on foot. They didn't know who I was then: it was just 'cause I was slabberin'. They went away and must have got photos of me and checked me out 'cause they came back and waited for me in the house. They took me out to the forest and broke my legs.

Psycho (age 20) had been on the run for a few months, boasting that "Psycho by name and Psycho by nature" somehow made him invincible and unable to be caught. Unfortunately, Psycho contracted appendicitis and had to have surgery. On the evening of his discharge from the hospital, he was recovering in his mother's home when the IRA broke down the door, dragged him from his bed, took him away, and shot him in the knees and ankles.

Tarring and Feathering

Initially, in the 1970s, the IRA used tar and feathers as a punishment, especially for girls dating British army soldiers.[40] This involved tying someone to a lamppost or railing, pouring hot tar or diesel oil over her, and then dousing her in feathers. The highest number of tarring and feathering incidents was recorded in 1972, when the total number came to twenty-eight.[41] A variant of tarring and feathering was to shave the offender's head, cover her in paint, and place a placard around her neck stating her offense. These punishments were intended to publicly shame the offender and were also an expulsion ritual. "Tarring and feathering was used with women consorting with the enemy, [it involved] shaming then beating then shooting." (Ex-prisoner F). Punished individuals knew that they were required to leave the area.[42]

In the 1970s, when the "no-go" areas for the police and army were firmly in place, an IRA punishment squad could afford the time and exposure that was involved in tarring and feathering someone.[43] Since the 1980s, as the security forces has increased their presence in Republican areas with random police and army patrols, and sophisticated surveillance equipment monitoring every move, the IRA has largely abandoned using paint, tar, and diesel oil to punish people. The whole procedure was becoming too time-consuming and conspicuous, and the IRA has resorted to this form of punishment only on rare occasions. One such instance was in 1995, when Denise Clarkin (age 16) was attacked. The following excerpt appeared in *The [Irish] Times* newspaper:

> Denise said the gang, who covered their faces with scarves, knocked at the front door. "I stood across the living room and one of them stuck a gun in my mouth and shouted, 'Get away from the door or I'll blow your brains out.'" Her parents, Brain and Margaret, tried to tackle the gang but one of the terrorists fired a blank at Mr. Clarkin. They then dragged Denise away. She said: "I was screaming and kicked one of them and he fell to the ground. They tied me to the lamppost and cut my hair. By that time Daddy and Mummy and some of the neighbours were running down the street and one of them shouted: 'Quick pour the paint over her.'"[44]

The IRA's decision to limit tarring and feathering of women was also influenced by the intervention of Derry Women's Aid, who accused IRA volunteers of sexism and misogyny.[45] The IRA, in part, heeded the message,[46] and incidents like the attack on Denise Clarkin have become extremely rare. In 2003 the INLA tarred and feathered two young teenagers ages 14 and 15 and claimed afterward that in doing so the victims had been treated more "empathetically" than they would have been by other organizations.[47]

Everything's Sweet: Post Traumatic Stress Disorder among the Hoods

The risks to the hoods' physical health are high, but so too are the emotional and psychological costs. One study examining the impact of receiving a PPA on the lives of a group of young people in West Belfast, with particular reference to their mental health, found that those who had been shot "exhibited very high levels of psychological distress and many symptoms of Post Traumatic Stress Disorder (PTSD)."[48] These symptoms consisted of intrusive reexperiencing, including flashbacks and dreams; avoidance; numbing reactions, including efforts to avoid thoughts or feelings associated with the trauma, for example minimizing the incident; a sense of a foreshortened future; and symptoms of increased arousal, including hypervigilance and difficulty in concentrating.[49] Furthermore Oscar Daly, a consultant psychiatrist who treats victims, argues that the factors that contribute to the hoods offending, such as inconsistent parenting and individual personality problems, may make it more difficult for them to recover from the trauma of the assault.[50]

Although no direct measures of PTSD were taken in this study, many of the hoods reported a mix of symptoms that indicated PTSD. Gerry (age 22) had been shot in both knees: "I'll hopefully make a full recovery from being shot—it depends on the bullet in my right leg. It causes me a lot of pain and I can't sleep at nights with it. I have a whole lot of nightmares where I relive what happened, and I break out in a cold sweat. I have to have a shower every morning."

The hoods' patterns of drug and alcohol dependency resulted from feelings of powerlessness and fear or as a way of escaping from these feelings. Although initial enquires would get the response that "everything's sweet," their substance abuse undoubtedly contributed to the mood swings they exhibited. Happy and excited one minute, and anxious and worried and depressed the next:

> I haven't got a life. Life's shit because of the way I get on in life. Gettin' a bad name, joyridin', takin' drugs, getting put out of the country, put on a curfew, a bad name, it sticks. They [local people] don't want to know me. I wanna get the "I wanna be the IRA" vigilantes off my back and be able to have a laugh with my mates without fuckin' up my head. The cost of it all is big trouble: the Provos comin' to the door and getting' a bad name. And I don't listen. It's dangerous: I could get killed or kill somebody else. I would like to be good and not have to look over my shoulder all the time. (Tim, age 17)

Jackie (age 17) spoke of her feelings of alienation and isolation:

> Everybody's depressed. Nobody wants to listen to young people like us, but we want somewhere to go, somebody to talk to, somebody we

can trust, but nobody wants to hear about it anyway. People in the past have always let you down. It all builds up until you say: "fuck it." You might try and talk to a friend or they might try and talk to you, but then your friend says she feels exactly the same way, and you don't know what to say to each other. You're scared to say that you're feeling suicidal in case people just tell you it'll be all right and don't listen to what you're sayin'. It's worse to say and not be listened to than not say at all. There's nobody out there for us.

Just over one third of the hoods interviewed in this research described suffering long periods of depression and having suicidal thoughts. Twenty-two percent admitted that they had attempted suicide at least once.[51] Angela (age 19) described a number of incidents when she self-harmed, trying to kill herself:

The last time was about seven months ago, and before that about three years ago. Life wasn't fair, and if I feel down or weak then somethin' stupid could happen. The first time was an overdose of Anadin. I took 47, second overdose of 65 Paracodal. Third time, I cut my throat with a glass bottle. The first time the tablets went missin' at the training school, so they asked another girl who told them that I took them. They took me to hospital to get my stomach pumped. The second time I was found unconscious by staff and had my stomach pumped. The third time I'd an argument with my girl. I was drunk and said I'd kill myself. She said: "Ahh you won't," dead cocky, so I smashed a Bacardi bottle and slashed it twice across my throat. There was a lot of blood and they were deep cuts. I wouldn't go to hospital. I said I'd bleed to death. I cut myself with razors in the arms, a couple of times on my head and legs. About five years, I've been doing it every day.

Tommy (age 23) first attempted suicide just after his mother died: "I took it bad when my mother passed away because I tried to kill myself. At times I'm all right, and other times I just wanna do myself in. I've tried to kill myself three times with paracetemols." Ryan, who at age 14 was the youngest of the hoods interviewed, admitted to frequently having thoughts of killing himself, either out of despair or for attention: "I might do somethin' to myself soon. Kill myself, and I'm scared of doin' it, puttin' my mind to it. I would do it. I can't help myself. If I've too much problems, I'll end up doin' it. I've tried it a couple of times, takin' tablets, do my wrists, wee nick on my wrist, tryin' to get attention. I'm really scared of doin' it, but I think I will." Danny had been taking a mixture of painkillers and sleeping pills when he attempted suicide one Friday night during the fieldwork period. He slit his wrists with a razor blade and narrowly missed slicing his tendons.

Although the instances of suicide following an attack are rare, William A. Thompson and Barry Mulholland conclude, "The actions of the paramilitaries seem to be part of a self-maintaining cycle . . . of fear, anger, revenge and a sense of having nothing to lose among the hoods."[52]

The hoods in this study lived lives characterized by danger and despair:

> I'm risking my life. If I crash, I'll kill myself, but if I do I hope I go fuckin' quietly, and I could kill someone else as well. I suppose when you look at it like that it's pretty stupid. My family worry about me killin' myself, and joyridin' isn't really getting' me what I want in life. It could cost me my life. It's just a matter of me taking a dodgy E and it killin' me. It puts me under pressure because I've no money, and then I go out and rob. My family didn't wanna know me 'cause I was taking Es and heroin. My life would be better if I just went out for a quiet drink and not take any drugs. (Danny, age 24)

The consequences of their behavior: imprisonment; exclusion from family and friends; pain and injury from accidents and PPAs; alcohol and drug overdoses; fear; isolation and premature death all mount up to a costly price for the thrills of a joyride or the escapism in a score. However, despite these costs, the hoods persist with their offending and antisocial behavior, and this remains the central puzzle of this book.

THREE

Search for Status

The hoods delinquency rivals that of young offenders in the rest of the United Kingdom and in the United States in terms of persistence and prevalence. In searching for an explanation for their behavior, this chapter has three aims: to place the hoods in the wider empirical context of the cultural and behavioral norms and values and the structural constraints of life in West Belfast; to explore the wider theoretical explanations of delinquency and highlight the degree to which these help us understand the hoods' behavior; and to delve more deeply into the relationships between the hoods and show how this has a profound effect on their behavior.

Status and Masculinity

The hoods in this study were all born in West Belfast, are from a working-class Catholic background, and are predominantly male. Their offending places them on the edge of local mainstream society, but they remain subject to structural constraints and social norms within their community, and they display some of the common values and characteristics associated with most residents in that area. To understand the hoods behavior, we first need a more general understanding of what is culturally expected of a man and how status is derived in this society.

In most societies, increased status is valued and sought after because it facilitates cooperation and access to social and economic resources. Thus, Jon Elster argues that it is a truism that "in all societies certain actions, achievements, possessions, or character traits are valued or seen as 'good,' bestowing 'honour' or 'glory' on those who display such 'goodness.'"[1] For Elster, examples of socially defined goodness include "the ability to suffer pain without showing it, courage in the face of danger, military prowess, wealth or learning, modesty and humility, beauty and strength."[2] The importance of any of these examples varies depending on the values and traditions of each society. Roger Petersen argues that status rewards carry more weight in closely knit, cohesive communities. He also states, "In communities where a rough equality of material conditions holds . . . the only way to become a 'big man' in the community may be through some sort of courageous action. This seems especially true for young males."[3]

West Belfast has high levels of social, economic, and political homogeneity. High levels of interaction and reciprocity among the population underpin the strong tradition of Republican and Nationalist ideology. While only a small proportion of the population have taken direct action based upon these values, many more adhere to them: "Republicanism is very strong, although most people aren't active, they would sympathise with it, and would be really proud to say 'I believe in the Republican cause and will give you my vote'" (Local Resident H). Traditional Republican ideology has emphasized, among other things, the notion of heroic self-sacrifice as necessary for the achievement of a United Ireland.[4] Since the 1970s, the preponderance of paramilitary groups, the armed presence of the security forces, and the resulting violence have sustained a prevailing sense of militarism and machismo.[5] This code extols the virtues of involvement in aggressive acts linked to civil and political unrest. In West Belfast, membership of the wider Republican Movement and in particular the IRA affords status. But, status is not necessarily about being liked or being popular, it is about being "respected and taken seriously by those around you."[6] This respect comes from being prepared to risk and/ or endure imprisonment, injury, and death for a political cause and from the willingness to use violence. As one resident put it, "If the Brits shot yer da' he's a hero. Even if he was just walkin' down the street and had never made a political statement in his life or done anything other than get up and go to work every day" (Community Worker L). Large crowds have turned out for funerals of IRA members and for Republican rallies commemorating those who have died. The reburial of Tom Williams in August 1999 brought West Belfast to a standstill, as 20,000 people took part in the memorial.[7] A content analysis of *An Phoblacht/Republican News* revealed the importance of commemorations, remembrances, and obituaries among supporters of the Republican Movement, and North and West Belfast are dotted with murals depicting the suffering of Republican heroes.[8] The hardships of the Blanket Protest that preceded the 1980 to 1981 Hunger Strikes have not been forgotten, and the Hunger Strikers have become martyrs,[9] their deaths honored with an annual parade through streets lined with black flags.[10] Such public commemoration spread beyond the boundaries of West Belfast when, in 2001, a wall mural commemorating the Hunger Strikes was painted in East Harlem, New York, by Gerard Kelly.[11]

Former prisoners are particularly prominent and influential. Having been convicted and imprisoned, they no longer need to hide their membership of the IRA and are the public face of the organization. Apart from membership in the Felons Club (a privilege reserved only for those Republicans who have been political prisoners and where portraits of the ten dead Hunger Strikers hang in the bar), this cadre continue their service to West Belfast through professional or voluntary community development work. One former prisoner, who served a thirteen-year sentence for attempted murder, argued that there are broadly similar reasons for joining the IRA and supporting a community mediation project:

> [T]he reason that people joined the IRA wasn't for personal gain. . . . It wasn't personal gain to be put in jail for ten or fifteen years, it wasn't personal gain to be shot dead, or maimed in an ambush. So, their reasoning for joining the IRA was to benefit the nationalist community that they came from. So, a lot of those people would be very community-orientated and would want to work within the community, and what better a way of helping the community than helping to resolve disputes within the community without having to resort to violence.

Many prisoners gained a formal education while in prison, which they would have been unlikely to have had the opportunity to pursue had they not been sentenced, and which complements their toughness and dedication.[12] This combination of skills enables many to have considerable informal power to shape opinions and establish directives on community issues:

> I'm a Republican and I know that I do command a certain amount of respect because of that and because people have seen that I'm

prepared to make sacrifices for my community. People all know me around here. I've lived here all my life and they know what my commitment to the community is. (Ex-prisoner V)

Others, who have not been prisoners, gain status by association: "People brag about stupid things and would say 'I personally know so and so [in the Republican Movement]' or 'I know them ones [Republicans] dead well.' It makes them feel important, you know to be able to say 'I can make a phone-call' or 'I'll get that sorted for you'" (Local Resident H).

It is estimated that in 1994, at the time of the cease-fire, total membership of the IRA was approximately five hundred. Even at its peak in the 1970s, membership is estimated to have been about 1,500.[13] The hoods are also small in number. Given that IRA members and hoods share similar traits, or place value on similar attributes—most obviously a willingness to take physical risks and a desire to attain some form of recognition or status through acts of aggression (although in the case of the IRA, recognition through acts of aggression is a by-product of their commitment to their political cause, not the primary intention)—it is plausible to suggest that some hoods could become IRA members. Although they may "share the same pond" as active Republicans, in general, their antisocial behavior excludes them from formal membership.

Recruitment into the IRA

The IRA's recruitment policies and practices have evolved in response to the changing political situation in Northern Ireland and the needs of the organization. In the 1970s, in reaction to the sectarian violence and presence of the British army on the streets of West Belfast, many Catholic young people zealously joined and fought for the IRA, playing a key role in street confrontations with the security forces.[14] The British government's policy of internment meant that every six weeks or so whole IRA battalions needed to be replaced. All volunteers were therefore readily accepted. Would-be recruits presented themselves to be vetoed by IRA intelligence officers, who would run background checks to ensure that they were not connected to the security forces in any way. Recruitment officers would take the new hopefuls through the IRA's rules and regulations, known as the Green Book, and judge whether they were suitable for active service. This process was aided if the young person had been a member of Na Fianna Eireann,[15] the IRA's youth wing. This organization aimed to encourage Republican values such as respect and a sense of belonging and commitment to the West Belfast community. It also operated like a youth club; a venue for young teenagers with some structured activities that would help to keep them out of trouble. An ex-prisoner explained how it worked:

> [Y]oung people coming through Na Fianna Eireann . . . at sixteen or seventeen they had the opportunity to join Sinn Féin, join the IRA, whatever part of the Republican family was about, or whatever they wanted. . . . There was no threat or formal obligation to join or stay with the Republican Movement after that. But that gave people a focus as well . . . especially when you had very little youth club provision in West Belfast, where all the funding for community groups was politically vetted, where there wasn't a big community infrastructure if you like to provide for community development things like that. So that was a focus for young people who didn't get into criminal behaviour. (Ex-prisoner L)

In the early 1980s, Loyalist paramilitaries exploded a bomb at a Republican funeral in the Ardoyne area of North Belfast, raising existing IRA suspicions that the organization had been compromised. The leak was traced to Na Fianna Eireann, and, according to Sinn Féin, further investigation revealed that the police had managed to penetrate deep into the IRA's youth wing. Na Fianna Eireann was disbanded, and it is believed that this had the unintended consequence of increasing delinquent behavior: "I'm not saying that every young person went into joyriding because Na Fianna Eireann wasn't there, but it was a thing that was missing then" (Ex-prisoner L). The demise of Na Fianna Eirann meant that the IRA had less direct contact with young people, who were disposed to risk taking and had fewer opportunities to channel that energy into what the IRA considered to be appropriate activities.

At this time, the IRA tightened up its recruitment practices. It became increasingly difficult to join the organization and, during the most recent cease-fire periods, it has become harder still. Members of the IRA were skeptical about the commitment of "cease-fire soldiers," believing that those who joined the organization during periods of relative peace wanted the benefits of belonging to the IRA, chiefly status, without having to bear the costs of risking their lives or their freedom. The process of joining the IRA became more protracted and was designed to eliminate both those who were not fully committed and to screen for potential informants. The IRA was not worried about infiltrators (the security forces or Loyalists), but it was concerned that some members might become police informants. Consequently, those with a previous history of antisocial behavior or drug dependency would not be accepted unless they could prove that they were no longer vulnerable to their previous habits. Thus, the vast majority of hoods were excluded from ever joining the IRA:

> They [the hoods] would have be a lot older and a lot more mature. Yes, there are some members [of the IRA] who people talk about saying "he's out battering joyriders and he was one himself," but there aren't many, and I wouldn't think any of this lot [the hoods in the research sample] would ever be accepted. (Ex-prisoner L)

This raises questions as to whether hoods aspire to become members of the IRA in the first place and whether their delinquency is a product of their frustration at not being a member?

The background to contemporary joyriding is to be found in the sectarian strife of the late 1960s and early 1970s:

> As paramilitary groups struggled for control they encouraged teenagers in the community to hijack cars. These cars, often burnt out, were used as diversions for the activity of the police. . . . Without doubt the excitement and sense of bravado derived from driving a hijacked car became attractive to some of these teenagers. . . . By the mid-seventies a recognisable stratum of joyriders had developed. These were young men who would steal cars in their own area, or close by and drive around recklessly for fun.[16]

Joyriding thus became a problem for the IRA when it slipped out of their control and, instead of successfully diverting the police, inadvertently drew them into West Belfast, at times disturbing IRA military operations.

Eric C. Schneider describes a similar relationship between an Italian-immigrant organized crime group and a youth gang called the Red Wings in East Harlem, New York, in the 1950s. The organized crime group protected the Red Wings and supported their attempts to keep rival Puerto Rican gangs out of the neighborhood, but "rumbles brought police and interfered with business and the Italian gangs were admonished to act defensively only."[17]

The hoods' attitudes toward the IRA were ambivalent. On the one hand, they were straightforwardly antagonistic: "They're dirty stinkin' bastards, the whole lot of them," according to Tony (age 24). Pete, a former hood, explained,

> There were two groups amongst us: those who chose to be one [a member of a paramilitary group] and those who didn't. They had power, but we didn't respect them. We saw them as 'monkeys.' It was very distinctly us and them, and they were mostly very stupid people controlled by a few very clever people.

O'Connor cites the example of a young person whose support for the IRA diminished after his first experience of joyriding: "I got into this stolen car one night, it was left up the back of the house, jumped into it and then drove it. Thought, it's better flying about in cars than getting in the rah and all, and I started stealing them and all, started hating the Provies [Provisional IRA]. They gave me a bad time" (Seán, age 15).[18] For Seán, joyriding offered more immediate excitement and gratification than joining the IRA, and he also became embittered.

On the other hand, some of the hoods expressed sympathy for the IRA's fighting role in the wider political conflict. A local community worker summed up this view:

> Their [the hoods'] view of the IRA is funny, in the sense that there is a dichotomy there, where on the one hand they despise the people who punish them who are members of the IRA or members of the Republican Movement, but on the other hand if there was some ambush on a police patrol or a British army patrol, they would be the first to come out and cheer it or applaud. You know, so there is that dichotomy in their thinking. . . . They do acknowledge and appreciate that at a

certain level the IRA are fighting a war of liberation, if you want, but on the other hand they're saying, "They're bastards because they punished me for what I'm doing." (Community Worker E)

The issue is further complicated for five of the hoods whose fathers were members of the IRA and for many more hoods who had strong Republican ties via family members. Aiden (age 18) refused to be specific when he spoke of his father's time in prison. He would say only that "he was in jail when I was younger for doing something worse than me. He tried to lecture me the other night when he was drunk, but I didn't listen to him. . . . He was a paramilitary, he's done time for paramilitary offences." Joe (age 18) admitted that he had "probably done things because he's [his father is] a Republican, he hates those things. I don't want anythin' to do with him. He's been looking for me with his mates with hammers. I've been doin' things to get at him, lettin' him know I've been in stolen cars."

Despite their personal connections, the IRA's strict recruitment criteria means that hoods, for the most part, cannot access this path to inclusion into the wider West Belfast community. This, in the minds of some community workers, is the reason why some young people became delinquent: "There were effectively no avenues or processes that allowed young people to move on in their lives, they were stuck in an unsatisfactory system. People can't participate in the community and [so they] went outside of it creating a subculture and expanded and developed it across West Belfast" (Community Worker F).

A Criminal Subculture?

Albert Cohen first used the phrase "delinquent subculture" to describe and explain delinquency among groups of young men in the inner cities.[19] Since then, British and American researchers have identified strong structural links between the social tradition and culture that young people grow up in and their subsequent behavior.[20] The suggestion is that membership in working-class subcultures demonstrates an essential sense of continuity with the parent culture.[21] A shared awareness of the limitations and restraints imposed by a poor job market, with its low pay, undesirable conditions, and insecurities, has led to a preoccupation with leisure roles, such as soccer, drinking, and offending. Rather than rejecting the dominant values and lifestyle, young people accommodate and assimilate these into their own behavior. Antisocial behavior and delinquency are viewed as part of the youths' adjustment to the subcultural context of underprivileged neighborhoods, where there is a clearly defined delinquent realm.[22]

This resonates with Leo Howe's argument that West Belfast residents have adapted culturally to the material necessities of the prevailing labor-market conditions. Employment in manufacturing is virtually nonexistent, and jobs in other sectors are very difficult to obtain. While jobs have declined in number, they have also declined in importance and status. Meanwhile, the practice of "doing the double" is morally acceptable and is seen as an astute and clever exploitation of the situation in order to get the best deal possible. Howe argues that unemployed people in West Belfast have not lost their commitment to work; rather they have modified the notion that households can be financed only by legitimate employment.[23] Given this customary involvement in illegal or illegitimate activities, Walter B. Miller's 1958 thesis—that "in manifesting itself as a one-sex peer group, the delinquent subculture is a variant of traditional working-class culture, and [. . .] delinquents are merely more involved with the 'focal concerns' of the adult parent culture: trouble, toughness, smartness and excitement"[24]—would seem applicable in part to the hoods in West Belfast. However, unlike the findings of these earlier studies, there is considerable tension and aggression between the hoods and adult males in West Belfast, which is manifested in violent vigilante action, the reporting of crime to the IRA, and hostile letters to the local paper, the *Andersonstown News*.

The hoods themselves spoke of this tension in terms of having lost their good name or reputation among the wider community. Tommy (age 23) said, "You'd have thought I'd two heads the way that people look at me. I feel like a bit of dirt and other people around my district haven't a good word to say about me apart from 'hoodin' cunt—you deserve all you get." Micky (age 18) argued, "I know I've lost my reputation.

People class me as a drug dealer, which I'm not. I'm always getting bad mouthed." Lisa (age 18) complained continuously that her neighbors were prejudiced against her: "I don't want to live in Turf Lodge 'cause if anything happens, I'll get the blame for it."

With no qualifications, a criminal record, and a dependency on drugs and/or alcohol, the hoods' chances of gaining and maintaining employment are very limited. Some, like Máire (age 16), who said she "wanted to get a job and then you can be somebody," are not impervious to the working-class image of the "good job." Likewise Joe (age 18) "would like to stop doin' it all, Comin' in here [YOC], getting' back into the community, look for a job to get money. Joinin' the job club or somethin', goin' to community centres to take me off the streets." Twenty-nine percent of the hoods had been in some form of full-time employment. These jobs, such as serving in fast food outlets or casual laboring, were of low status, even by working-class standards, and in most cases they had opted out of the joint middle- and skilled working-class value system, which holds to the principle that work is central to living, and which upholds virtues such as "bettering oneself" or accepting one's station in life as a person who is low-waged and unskilled. The hoods in this study became unemployed because of boredom, feeling debased, and believing that there is little financial benefit in labor. Sammy (age 18) lost his job "because of not turnin' up and drinkin' at lunchtimes." Tony (age 24) "didn't like being subordinate and I had a bad attitude. I didn't like the boss so I grabbed him round the neck and then I was fired."

Based on observations of working-class young people in London in the early 1960s, David Downes describes this process, whereby young people disconnect themselves from middle-class educational and occupational aspirations and practices, as "dissociation." This process "constitutes neither frustration nor alienation, but conformity with their allotted low social and economic station in life."[25] For example, according to Neil (ex-hood, age 29): "Education, employment and all that was always something that other people did, it was never really an option for me and I never had any sense that it was taken away, it was just never really an option." Thus, as Dick Hobbs puts it, "the more dissociated the youth will become, the more he will try to recoup in the sphere of leisure the freedom, achievement, autonomy, and excitement that are unavailable at work."[26] Rather than suffering from frustrated ambition at not being able to access the labor market, the hoods behavior and attitudes mirror Downes's description of dissociated working-class youth in 1960s London, where delinquency was "principally hedonistic, focused on drinking, fighting and malicious damage to property, rather than instrumentally turned towards the accumulation of wealth."[27]

However, the hoods' inability to access both "legitimate" law-abiding and "illegitimate" law-violating groups prevents them from gaining any form of recognized prestige and the accompanying resources. Richard Cloward and Lloyd Ohlin described young men who failed to attain admission to either a law-abiding or a law-violating group as the "double failures," who would, it was conjectured, give up and become drug users and hustlers.[28] Furthermore, status, as we shall see, is gained in other ways. The hoods behavior exhibits a set of norms and values that sets them apart from the rest of West Belfast society but does not dislocate them entirely. They are not impervious to the prevailing culture or to the expectations and ambitions of those around them. Evidence for this is clearly seen in their relationships with their families.

Family Relations

Running throughout the hoods' accounts of their antisocial behavior was the theme of family breakdown both as a cause and as a consequence of their delinquency and about which the hoods expressed anger and regret. Jackie (age 17) said, "Nobody had a stable mummy and daddy and the community is away in the head. There is not one family that I know that is stable and gives the child stability and love. . . . Everybody thinks this society is normal but it isn't—it's fucked up. Parents don't know how to react to it and get out of it." An unstable family environment, and/or inconsistent parenting, is a predictive factor in delinquency.[29] Half of the hoods' parents remained married to each other, but those who grew up with absent fathers were keen to vent their anger and bitterness:

> My da doesn't even send me a birthday card or nothin'. He's a fuckin' asshole. The way it is now, I don't give a fuck, he's never shown any affection to me so why should I show it to him. The next time I see

him I'm goin' to say "you're a fucking shithead, you asshole." (Paul, age 16)

I haven't talked to him in six or seven years. I'm not fussed about him, couldn't see him being of any benefit. He's a bit of a dickhead. He fucked off and left my ma with six kids. He's not thinkin' about us and I wouldn't want to know him. If I met him I'd wanna hit him with a big plank of wood and ask him why he split, but I wouldn't go lookin' for him. (Mark, age 19)

Even though Angela's (age 19) father now lives at the end of her street, she said, "I don't see him, he doesn't come this way. I don't miss him. I only met him about five years ago. He was in jail, he was caught with bombs—in for 14 years. I didn't miss him."

Paul, Mark, and Angela had particular complaints about their parents, but almost all of the hoods reported very poor family relationships. One clear reason for this was their victimization of their own parents. Colin (age 17) stole his father's car, and the theft has remained a point of contention: "I ask my ma and da for money, scrounge, steal . . . I stole his car. I feel guilty because he reminds me of it from time to time. . . . I would like him to just forget about it." Marty (age 20) admitted to manipulating his mother: "I can be nice to her if I'm lookin' for money. . . . I don't tell her the truth and it's not difficult for me to do this." Steve's (age 18) mother "asks me to stop stealin' and I tell her I do, but I don't stop. When I see her she slabbers away; I don't really listen to her." Nick's (age 17) parents no longer trust him:

Everywhere I go they're watchin' me. My mother lifts her purse when I'm around. They always keep a check on their money. My father doesn't trust me around money at all 'cause I'm a known thief. I'm a fucking kleptomaniac accordin' to my father. . . . She [mother] doesn't trust me—she never did, well not that much. She definitely doesn't respect me anymore. Everyday she warns me about my behaviour, telling me not to fuck about. . . . My father really doesn't trust me.

Brendan's (age 17) father became increasingly desperate to change his son's behavior:

I don't like him [father] and he doesn't like me. He doesn't like me 'cause I'm a hood and a thief. I've never liked him. He says nothin' to me he's a big lazy sad thing, just lies about and is borin'. He shouts at me and says that he "will break my legs the next time I catch you in a stolen car." I just walk out of the house.

Likewise, when Sean's (age 17) mother discovered he was dealing drugs "she cracked up. . . . She smacked me across the face" and Eamon's (age 18) mother's response was to throw him out of the family home: "When I've been joyridin' and I come in and she [mother] fucks me out 'til I wise up, so I don't come in with too much drink in me. She's thrown me out about seven times, drink inside me nearly every time. I come in drunk, spend the housekeepin,' and we argue." Máire's (age 16) father called in Social Services, who placed her in a care unit:

> I don't talk to him at all 'cause of the drugs; I choose drugs over my family. He's against them, doesn't like them at all. When he found out he was cut up; he was in bad form. He gave me a chance at first, but I kept takin' them. He then put me into care, he did it to me to try and stop me takin' them. I was doin' other things as well, joyridin', stealin', hangin' about. I hate him 'cause he's a dick. He does my head in. I can't do nothin' and he wants to know about it. Always finds out about it. Everybody tells him what you don't want him to know. . . . The two of them think I'm a scumbag—that's what they call me.

Liam (age 21) described how, in West Belfast's close-knit communities, parents of hoods suffer a collapse in good relations with their neighbors: "For the families there is a big shame thing—people would get shouted at in the street and if an argument broke out people would just say, "What would you know, your son's a fuckin' joyriding hood." Letters to the local newspaper provide more evidence of parents being blamed. For example, "[I]f you don't know where your 15 or 16-year-old is at 2 am then you are part of the problem."[30] Parents, however, were often at a loss as to how to influence their children's behavior. Following a crash in a stolen car that killed her son Brian, who was joyriding with friends, and two passengers in the car that they hit, Carmel Donnelly described life with her son in the years before his death:

> People seemed to think that the parents were to blame. There is this great theory that we are all lying drunk somewhere. I had a social life before he started, but we would have walked and drove through the

area all the time trying to find Brian and bring him in. I talked to any-one who I thought could help. Social workers, educational experts, everyone. We were not living anymore: we were existing. . . . Looking back I can't believe everything that we went through. Our lives be-came a battle.[31]

Most parents, like Alex's (age 19) mother, would be deeply upset if the police searched their home: "She's looking for an excuse now to throw me out of the house. She wants me to get my own place. I can't talk to her now. She doesn't listen to me because the cops done over the house and found everything, blow and all." In West Belfast "bringing trouble to the door" in the form of the police or Sinn Féin and the IRA is a particular shame. A visit from the police is a very public event. Plain-clothes detec-tives accompanied by at least one police Land Rover and, perhaps, de-pending on the area and the political climate at the time, army support, may descend upon the family home. Armed and uniformed police and army personnel scout around the house, crouching at the end of gardens, guns resting on their knees or in the crook of their arm in case of attack. Families fear being maligned because their child was the cause of an un-desirable security presence on their street: "bringing peelers [the police] to the door, gives you a bad name, cops callin' to the house" (Shane, age 17). Neighbors also feel tainted by their proximity to hoods, and are concerned that other residents may think that the unwanted attention has something to do with them.

Of even more concern to the family is a visit from the IRA. Although much more discreet, news of their call quickly spreads, and the effect can be devastating to a family: "She [mother] always cries because of what I am doin' and because people keep comin' to the door. Then my da shouts at her 'cause he thinks that she can't control me" (Shane, age 17). If a young person has been placed on a curfew or excluded, parents have to endure more than one visit: "He [father] threw me out of the house, and he doesn't talk to me because I got thrown out of the coun-try. He was cracking up because the IRA was coming to the door. I see him but he doesn't talk to me" (Steve, age 18). Community Worker P explained that "the parents often take the threat on board more seriously than the young person and deal with it on a day-to-day basis, fearing for their son's lives and their quality of life. There is a taboo on the family name in the district." There have been reports that parents of hoods will pay money to neighbors who allege that damage has been done to their property, rather than risk their child being reported to the IRA.[32]

Bringing the IRA to the door is particularly difficult for fathers. In such a male-dominated culture, having a child who is a hood implies that they have failed in their duty, reflecting some weakness or lack of manliness, and necessitating the intervention of a more authoritative group to assume the responsibility of disciplining the child. Eugene's (age 19) father's feelings of shame were amplified because he supported the IRA and held its members in high regard: "He likes the IRA and I don't—this is the main conflict."

While Sinn Féin insisted that home visits were merely part of their investigation and information-gathering procedures, hoods like Dessie (age 18) argued that these calls amounted to intimidation:

> I would worry about her [Dessie's mother] because the IRA held her and my dad hostage when they came looking for me. [They] held her for an hour when I wasn't there. I wouldn't want her to be hurt; she's had to go to the doctor and get tablets because of her nerves. I feel bad about that because it's me that has put her through it. I'm responsible for it.

Some families can be subjected to these experiences for years as younger children grow up to mimic the antisocial behavior of their older siblings. Recalling the IRA coming to his house when he was 5 years old, Conner (age 19) said, "I grew up thinking fuck the rah and just do it." He claimed he watched them put a gun to his mother's head because his two older brothers were hoods.

Davy (age 17), whose legs were broken by the IRA for defying his exclusion order, blames them just as bitterly for terrorizing his mother: "Before they done me, they were following my ma about the streets. She was dead scared as well. She was terrified of something happenin' to her. They didn't have to follow her to get to me, they could have got me anytime . . . 'cause me ma didn't do anything on them."

Fear and anxiety takes its toll. Gerry (age 22) believed that his kneecapping triggered his mother's heart attack, but she also suffered from a number of other ailments: "She was sad and angry when I got shot and she worries about me. She has arthritis, high blood pressure and a weak heart, and I worry about her in case she hurts herself." Martin (age 17) said his behavior had given his mother high blood pressure, and she was "sick with worrying." He continued, "I've put her though hell—so she says. . . . I told her things like drug dealin' and takin' drugs, she just started cryin'. . . she says 'you don't understand the pressure you're putting me under with the rah watchin' the house.' The street wants me and my brother out of Ballymurphy."

The loss of trust between a hood and his parents is often irreparable, but there were some cases of parents publicly supporting their offspring. Paul (age 19) spoke of his good relationship with his mother: "Me and my mum, the two of us get along dead on. We talk a lot about takin' drugs and me quietin' down and getting' a job. It hurts her that I take drugs and steal cars. I feel she knows what I'm goin' through. We can have a joke with each other. She helps me a lot, buys me drink, gives me money for blow." When he was accused of being a drug dealer and ordered to leave Poleglass after slogans appeared on the walls of houses in the development such as "BURNS OUT—ALL OUT" and "DRUG DEALERS OUT", his mother defended him in the local newspaper: "[H]e is not a drug dealer. . . . I'm not saying he was a total saint but he didn't deal drugs. If I found out he was I'd break his legs myself."[33]

Mick (age 20) felt he could rely on his father if he needed him:

> I don't talk to him [father] but I would if I'd a problem with the paramilitaries and when I was thrown out of school, he was runnin' about all over the place tryin' to get me back in. If it hadn't been for him, I would've been shot by the IRA—I know that he'll always be there for me if I need him. Bringin' the peelers to the door does his head in. He said, "No son of mine will be getting shot while I'm still alive."

His mother also paid off his drug debt: "When I was sellin' drugs, I owed £150 to the man I was buying from, and I told my ma and she gave me the money for it." Drug dealers in Northern Ireland, like creditors generally, get very upset if their debtors do not pay what they owe.

PEER RELATIONS

There is a general consensus that peer influence is extremely important in adolescence.[34] Nicholas Emler and Stephen Reicher argue, however, that such a claim "concurs with popular stereotype, informal observation and some research evidence, but it is a description of social relations and adolescence, not an explanation."[35] It remains unclear whether having delinquent peers causes an individual to offend or whether delinquent young people gravitate toward like-minded people who are delinquent. That said, the nature of the hoods' relationships among themselves provides important clues to understanding why they persist in offending despite the threat of PPAs.

Street life, for most hoods, begins with abusing solvents at age nine or ten. The resultant poor school attendance (54 percent had been excluded from school, mostly between the ages of 12 and 14,[36] and the rest simply dropped out) and association with other children involved in delinquency precipitates further offending that intensifies with age. Thus, once someone voluntarily embarks on one course of action (for example, solvent abuse and underage drinking), that person soon becomes involved in unanticipated offending (for example, shoplifting) as a means to sustain that action.

For younger children playing in the street, the joyriders' antics provide entertainment and excitement, and the abandoned or burnt-out cars often become temporary playgrounds. Some of these children learn to break into vehicles before they are in their teens, and before long they graduate to hotwiring the car to get it to start. If they have the necessary tools, the hoods estimated that they could steal a car within sixty seconds, while those with less experience act as lookouts. Youth Worker P explained, "There is a definite culture of it [offending] and now it's 7- to 8-year-olds doing what the older ones are doing and tagging along. They know what they are doing, but they don't understand the consequences of what they're doing. It's fun, exciting, the thrill of the chase." Once these young people are tall enough for their feet to reach the control pedals, they start to drive. Sammy (age 18) said, "I started gettin' into cars when I was 14 or 15 and just raked [drove] about. After about 16 I started to steal 'em to sell on as well as drivin' 'em about." As in the case of the burglars in Richard T. Wright and Scott H. Decker's study in St Louis, Missouri, having elected to participate in street life sets up young hoods for further offending "as part of the natural flow of events."[37]

Hooding also results from a wish to emulate or to avenge older siblings. There were four different sibling groups in the sample, and at one point during the fieldwork four members of one family were all under threat from the IRA for joyriding and vandalism. The slogan daubed in paint on a shop front in Andersonstown reading "[family name] OUT" could have referred to any one of three male siblings and their sister. Connor described how the IRA had forced his family from their home because of the antisocial behavior of his older brothers. His justification for becoming a hood was retaliation for his family's victimization by the IRA: "the rah tortured my family, and now I'm torturing the rah."

Are the Hoods a Gang?

Headlines in the local newspapers such as "Gang attacks cars and school minibus during 'drug-inspired' rampage" indicate, that as far as the general public is concerned, the hoods are thought to be a gang.[38] It was very clear from the interviews and field observations that almost all of the hoods' delinquency was carried out with at least one other person. Even in situations when only one hood steals a car, others quickly become involved. The joyrider looks for groups of other young people gathered on the street so that he can be observed driving the stolen car.

These young people hang out together because they share interests and they have fun together. When Julie's (age 16) friends call round for her in a stolen car, she gets in "because it's good and you get a good laugh. I don't get in a car when I don't want to." Likewise Marty (age 17) said, "[W]hen I see my friends goin' out every week I wanna go out too, so I drug-deal to get money to go out and then I don't come home. I stay out all night getting' into mischief, gettin' into things I shouldn't be doing." Although the costs of these friendships can be high, their lure is strong. Sammy (age 18) had been warned by the IRA that if he was caught joyriding again he would be kneecapped for a third time. He took this warning seriously but was worried that his good friend, who was due to be released from the YOI, would persuade him to get into a stolen car. His prediction was correct, and he was spotted joyriding with this friend some weeks later.

When the behavior is no longer fun or is too costly, young people move on and find new groups of friends. Liam (age 21) went to school with five of the hoods and considered them to be friends but he didn't enjoy their activities: "I would never disown friends that got involved but I would never do it myself. They'd give me a hard time for not playin' the game, try to make out like there's somethin' wrong with me, but I didn't care. In the end I just stayed away from them and that's why I'm not a hood." Gary (age 17) recalled that it was "just the wrong crowd. I stopped hangin' around with them. Found new mates and now I only get into trouble sometimes—vandalism, fightin' just stupid things. But with this last crowd I'd be sittin' in a stolen car watchin' them burn a house. The past few weeks I haven't got into anything like the trouble I used to." Finding new friends can be difficult, but Joe (age 18) considered it necessary if he were to stop offending: "[I]f I got other people to hang around with I'd not hang around with people who've no jobs and are fuckin' about."

In the United States, research on street gangs in urban settings has yielded a distinction between gangs and other delinquent youth who group together.[39] There is a consensus that gangs "are not just networks of delinquent friends but that they are different and special."[40] Some authors use the criminal behavior to specify this difference[41] and others focus more on the organizational structure and activities as a means of defining the gang. Thus Martín Sánchez Jankowski, in his study of thirty-seven street gangs in three metropolitan areas in the United States over a ten-year period, defines a street gang in the following way:

> an organized social system that is both quasi-private (not fully open to the public) and quasi-secretive (much of the information concerning its business remains confined within the group) and one whose size and goals have necessitated that social interaction be governed by a leadership structure that has defined roles; where the authority associated with these roles has optimized to the extent that social codes

are operational to regulate the behaviour of both the leadership and the rank and file; that plans and provides not only for the social and economic services of its members, but also for its own maintenance as an organization; that pursues such goals irrespective of whether the action is legal or not; and that lacks a bureaucracy (i.e., an administrative staff that is hierarchically organized and separate from leadership).[42]

Not all gang researchers agree with Jankowki's emphasis on formal organizational structure,[43] but there is consensus that some sense of pulling together is crucial to the existence of a gang. Sudhir Venkatesh describes how the Black Kings in the Robert Taylor housing project in Chicago in the 1980s, used terms like "family," "nation," and "black brotherhood" in conversation to cultivate group cohesion and to emphasize "a shared mission and to lend meaning to their activities."[44] Failing that, the Black Kings also used fines and physical assault to "ensure solidarity." The hoods in this study did speak of "them and us" when referring to the IRA, the police, or even local law-abiding residents. Most of them acknowledged that those they associate with are also hoods and accepted the label "hoods." However this label is a descriptive expression rather than an insignia. There is no organization known as "the hoods," no hierarchical structure exists, and there are no distinctive initiation ceremonies.

Street gangs are also defined by their sense of territory. There are smaller bands of hoods who associate themselves with the various housing developments and neighborhoods, but there was no evidence during the fieldwork of a spirited and sustained defense of territory among other hoods of a type that could be described as a turf war.

Public allegiance to an identifiable group that has some central governance is crucial to a gang's existence, but it is important not to overemphasize the extent to which gangs are cohesive and homogenous. Members of street gangs are diverse in outlook and attitude, and rather than have a consistent and strong leadership, the groups are often described as being internally unstable and "must continually reach consensus in order to act in a collective manner."[45] However, when faced with opposition from a rival gang or the police, it is expected that the gang will become much more cohesive and act in a much more collective fashion.[46]

The hoods are not a unified group, nor have they become more cohesive in the face of opposition from the IRA. Instead, they have remained in their loose and disorganized state, acting independently or in small cliques of two or three and taking part in what Jankowski describes as "ad hoc collective behaviour."[47] This familiar pattern has been identified in many studies of delinquency. Early work describes "amorphous coalitions of cliques,"[48] and "groups with loose 'ties' and limited cohesion" were also noted.[49] A general concept of "network," where there is some regularity among interactions but notions of membership are extremely vague, better fits the hoods' ties to one another.

Martin Gold characterized the behavior of a group of young offenders in Flint, Michigan, as a "pickup game."[50] Similarly, the way in which hoods cluster together is comparable to groups of people who come together for impromptu games of soccer in the park after work or on the weekend. There will be some regulars and some who will appear infrequently, but whoever turns up can play. There is no exclusion of the kind that gangs apply to nonmembers. Often strangers will join in, and players may phone their friends and cajole them into coming to play. They are not territorial, unlike most gangs, and if their usual "pitch" is occupied, they will find somewhere else close by and throw down bags and clothing to act as make-shift goal posts. They are not a soccer team, they do not have a name, and there is no prerequisite level of skill or fitness in order to play.

In much the same way, the hoods come together to play, except their games involve joyriding and other antisocial behaviors. Like soccer or basketball, these games necessitate certain skills in order to be played well, and for the duration of the game a skillful player is highly regarded among the other participants. Furthermore, this respect for a good player often extends beyond the confines of the game, because sporting ability or gamesmanship is viewed as a sign of other positive and not directly observable traits. Those with sporting talent are applauded for their skills, and their popularity and influence increases. Professional soccer players get paid thousands of pounds, gain lucrative sponsorship deals, and marry beautiful women. The good amateur Saturday morning player is thought of as a "good bloke" and is bought drinks in the pub after the game. The joyrider in West Belfast is applauded for his skill and audacity and gains the esteem of his peers.

Whereas the soccer players meet together for the sole purpose of playing their game, Gold argues that there is little planning behind specific delinquent events.[51] For some hoods, like Lisa (age 18), "Trouble just happens, I don't know why it happens. If I go into a shop and there is somethin' there that I can take, I'll just take it." Such hoods exhibited little evidence that their behavior was premeditated. Most, however, acknowledged that going out with their friends meant getting into trouble: "I suppose it wouldn't make any difference who I was with, it's me that does what I'm doing, nobody's twistin' my arm," says Pat (age 19).

The IRA has been the most powerful organization in West Belfast for over thirty-five years, commanding considerable financial resources, an arsenal of weapons, a ready supply of skilled volunteers, and the support of many local residents. If the hoods were to become more organized and act in a collective, strategic manner operating, for example, protection rackets or a drug distribution business, this would put them in direct conflict or at least possible competition with the IRA. The IRA has proven its strength in West Belfast on many occasions by virtually eliminating rival paramilitary organizations such as the Irish People's Liberation Organization (IPLO) and disabling the INLA.[52] Therefore, one explanation as to why the hoods are not an organized gang lies in the strength of the IRA in West Belfast. As autonomous individual agents, the hoods, who come together in an ad hoc fashion and do not profess loyalty to anyone other than their closest associates, have greater flexibility and safety than they would have if they were more organized and visible.

Jankowski argues that American street gangs provide members with two key forms of protection: personal anonymity, as an individual gets subsumed into the identity of the group, and personal physical protection. He suggests that young people who join a gang are "either tired of being on the alert or want to reduce the probability of danger to a level that allows them to devote more time to their effort to secure more money."[53] Without a more formal gang structure to regulate their behavior and to insulate and protect them, the hoods are vulnerable to the wider community, as noted by a community worker who focuses on young people under paramilitary threat: "They are an easily recognised group, totally isolated from the rest of the community, unemployed and drinking cider on the street corner. Ninety-six percent of them are unemployed, the criminal justice system discriminates and isolates them, and they are scapegoated by the community. It really isn't fair, as they are such easy targets—I mean who cares about them?" The hoods also spoke about feeling vulnerable to local people: "[T]he community don't like me at all, handbrakin' in stolen cars in the early hours of the mornin', standin' at corners drinkin' and slabberin'. They'd rather see me dead than out of there [Young Offenders Institute]. They went to the paramilitaries tellin' 'em I was standin' drinkin'," said Joe (age 18).

Although strongly attached to street life, the hoods in this sample were not committed to their families or to one another. Their friendships were loose and volatile, with very little loyalty. As Kelly (age 17) put it, "Nobody trusts anybody. It's like a cat and mouse game out there." Pete, an ex-hood, described all of his former associates as "treacherous, back-stabbing bastards" and told how on a night out people would try to steal each other's drinking money: "[I]t was every man for himself, and if your friends get in the way, then tough." In their study of burglars in St. Louis, Missouri, Wright and Decker also uncovered little evidence of trust or loyalty among the offenders:

> The predominant sentiment among them was "you have to look after number one." These offenders did not even pay lip service to the importance of upholding any code of "honor amongst thieves." . . . Most of the burglars conducted their affairs without regard for the feelings of others; when the chips were down even friends and associates were liable to be judged as fair game in any sort of money-making scheme.[54]

In West Belfast, this lack of trust and loyalty among the hoods is counterbalanced by the normative ideal that under no circumstances must they inform on each other. This is in line with the IRA's attitude toward informants to the police and the British army: "You can't tell anything, if it goes round and your mates find out . . . you just can't" (Alex, age 18). However, when under pressure, hoods do give information to both the police and the IRA. An example of this is Gerry (age 22), whose betrayal occurred when he was kneecapped for the burglary of an IRA member's house. One of his alleged accomplices had been on the run from the IRA for some time, and had moved to England in order to escape being knee-capped. When he tried to return to Belfast, his father visited Gerry, who admitted that during his interrogation he gave the IRA the first name he thought of, sentencing the man's son to certain punishment. On hearing about this betrayal, Gerry's father was so angry by the additional disgrace and shame that his son had brought on the family that he physically attacked his son. Not only was Gerry a hood, but also a "tout" who had informed on an innocent person. Gerry's friends avoided him and while one or two of the young women felt sorry for him, the rest despised him.

The hoods share behavior with gang members—they steal, they are violent, and they use drugs—but they do not have a collective identity, an organizational structure with assigned roles and activities, or a sense of loyalty to a larger group that is recognizably gang-like.

So far, this book has presented a descriptive account of the hoods' behavior, which amounts to "a big, big game and all about who can play the game the best," as in the words of Pete, an ex-hood. As we have seen, playing this "game" has serious physical and emotional consequences for those who take part, and it would appear to the outside observer that there is not much to be gained from getting involved. Yet most of the hoods continue undeterred and with enthusiasm. This anomaly has presented the most puzzling questions still to be addressed: why do the hoods continue to offend in this manner and why do PPAs not prevent the hoods from reoffending? Although the hoods' behavior appears to have limited utility, analysis of the fieldwork data uncovered a rationale governing their actions. The next chapter will argue that the hoods' ability to play the "game" well sends out signals or indications of desirable qualities to other hoods, and the possession of these traits has specific rewards. Deciphering these signals and rewards provides the key to understanding the hoods' persistent antisocial behavior, despite the severe costs that are directly incurred.

FOUR

Signaling Games

So far, this book has presented a descriptive account of the hoods' behavior, which was described by Pete, a former hood who is now a community worker, as being a "big game and all about who can play the game the best." Playing this game risks serious physical injury and imprisonment, and it would appear to the outside observer that while the costs of participating are relatively high, there is not much to be gained from being involved.

A closer analysis of the interview data reveals two main themes: first, that hoods reminiscent of burglars described by Wright and Decker see "their fate as inextricably linked to their ability to fulfill the imperatives of life on the street,"[1] and second, that a key imperative was toughness. As Pete went on to say, "There was an unwritten rule—to try to be the best hood that you could possibly be. 'Real power' on the streets lay with being the best hood—being mad, bad, and game." These terms "mad," "bad," and "game" encompass the hoods' activities. "Mad" and "game" imply behavior that is essentially expressive or for display, and "bad" involves behavior that is more instrumental. Therefore, to be "mad" is to be crazy and as wild and outrageous as possible. "Mad" behavior appears irrational or foolish, such as high-speed joyriding and excessive drinking and drug use. The word "bad" is associated with activities that are nasty and tough, for example, being violent, engaging in vandalism, selling drugs, and undermining people. Finally, "game" is being prepared to take any risk and to accept any challenge, such as starting a fight with a much stronger opponent. Once again, Pete put it very succinctly: "It's a big game and all about who can play the game the best—how mad you are how hard you are. You could be stupid, ugly, poor but you got status from being 'game.'"

In an environment where access to both the conventional "legitimate" and "illegitimate" routes to gaining prestige is extremely limited, status is attained through criminal prowess. This association between status and criminal prowess and toughness leads to the hypothesis that these young people are engaged in a costly signaling game in order to establish and maintain their status among their peers.

Signaling Status

One possible way of explaining behavior that exacts a high cost in terms of risk or resources in return for a relatively small reward is to use the game-theory concept of signaling. That is, to view the behavior as a signal intended to communicate information about the signaler to another party, the receiver. This information is usually some form of private information such as the possession of an attribute or characteristic like toughness, commitment to a cause, or honesty.[2] These attributes are not directly observable but are understood by the signaler and the receiver to be highly correlated with the behavior that is being displayed. Signaling of this type is most likely to occur in social contexts where there is incomplete information or an asymmetry of information between the signaler and the receiver. That is, the signaler knows if he or she truly possesses the attribute while the receiver can only estimate the likelihood that this person does, based on how convincing the signal is. While most of the time it benefits the signaler and the receiver to communicate honestly, there are some individuals or mimics who will try to deceive the receiver by signaling that they possess a particular property when, in fact, they do not. In order to discern accurately between the honest signaller and the mimic, the receiver needs to pay close attention to the costs associated with producing the signal. Only someone who truly possesses the property will be willing to bear the cost of the behavior.

Not all signals are costly. For example, there are some signals or cues such as skin color or gender that the signaler effortlessly displays, because they are there anyway. If taxi drivers believe being female is a sign of being a safe fare, then a female passenger does not have to expend any extra energy to convince a taxi driver to pick her up. A male passenger, on the other hand, cannot fake being female without considerable effort. Given that all he wants is a taxi ride home, he is probably not willing to make the effort to pass convincingly as a woman, and so may decide to invest in other less costly signs of decency, such as being well dressed or hailing a taxi in an affluent area in order to ensure he gets a ride.[3]

Signaling theory's origins are in economics and evolutionary biology. Michael Spence's seminal research on job market selection[4] and Amotz Zahavi's influential work on mate selection in the animal world[5] introduced these ideas, which have been applied widely in economics,[6] biology,[7] and more recently in anthropology[8] and sociology.[9]

The Conditions for Signaling

There are two primary conditions for costly signaling to be present. First is that there are mutual benefits to be gained from truthful communication and second is that the actors operate in a low-trust environment where information is scarce and unequally distributed.

The first condition, that there are mutual benefits to be gained from truthful communication, is met within the context of relationships among the hoods, which are both competitive and cooperative. They compete with one another to gain and maintain their status, but they also cooperate on criminal enterprises and in protecting one another from being caught by the paramilitaries and the police. The absence of a formal gang organization such as is found elsewhere in the United Kingdom and in North America is also crucial. In these more hierarchical structures, members are assigned a rank associated with a certain authority. Without a hierarchical gang structure to guarantee their reputation, hoods regularly need to communicate or prove their toughness and criminal prowess to others. But why is such a reputation important? Given that monetary gain from the hoods' activities is minimal, respect and recognition appear as larger incentives for their criminal activity. In the parochial and insular world of the street, a lack of respect leaves a hood vulnerable to physical attack and limits his access to the resources and knowledge he needs not only to survive in West Belfast but also to exploit reputation-enhancing opportunities. On the basis of such notoriety, other hoods will be more likely to share information and cooperate on criminal enterprises that are risky and require a degree of trust among all those involved. If successful, these enterprises can have limited financial rewards and the risks further enhance a hood's status. If unsuccessful, they risk imprisonment and a PPA. Knowing another hood's type is therefore crucial if one is to survive and thrive in this environment.

West Belfast has often been described as a "close-knit community," but after years of conflict, surveillance, and countersurveillance, residents are cautious as to who to trust and what information to reveal. Republicans, in particular, have always felt vulnerable to infiltration by the British Secret Service, and being an informer or a 'tout' can carry a death sentence. The murder of senior Sinn Féin member Denis Donaldson in April 2005 after he was exposed as a British secret agent serves as a reminder of this. The hoods, alienated from a mainstream society where trust is already low, and without a formal gang structure to protect them from the IRA or other hoods, find themselves in a very low-trust environment where good information is scarce and unequally distributed. According to one community worker, "A lot of people who think they are under threat aren't, they are just paranoid" (Case Worker, Base 2). This might be because of a lack of good information in an environment where rumors abound, or it could be that hoods exaggerate the threat against them to enhance their status. Either way, the overall effect is to amplify their distrust: "They're all nosy fuckers in my street so I can't really do anything. There are only two people I don't hate. I got caught on video selling cannabis, some nosy fuck videoed me. I know who it was and I'll get them eventually" (Georgie, age 21).

Despite these high levels of distrust, hoods do not act alone, and to co-operate effectively they must trust one another, both to keep information confidential and to carry out their part of whatever bargain has been made. When it comes to offending, if one informs, the others get caught. On the run from the police and/or the IRA, they have to rely on their friends and associates in order to remain safe and free, despite being aware that when under pressure hoods, like Gerry (age 22) admitted, "will just say the first name that comes into [their] heads." Establishing another's trustworthiness is thus vital to their survival. In the following sections I will explore the evidence in support of three key predictions from signaling theory: 1) that tough hoods are recognized for their status; 2) that the behavior displayed is closely related to the underlying property being conveyed; and 3) that hoods have effective ways of broadcasting their behaviors.

1. Tough Hoods Are Recognized for Their Status

For the hoods, notions of prestige and reputation do not imply adherence to a moral code or aspirations toward something higher or more upright. These young people aspire to feel good about themselves and to have the good opinion or esteem of their friends and associates. This reputation comes from being tough and violent, and in adopting an attitude that cares little for one's own safety or the safety of others. It is dependent upon their exploits and is built up over time. There is also a system of ranking within the group, which is never explicitly stated, and so there is no official leader, but the hoods appeared to know implicitly who was the toughest. Pete (ex-hood), for example, recalled that "[t]here were eight to 12 of us in my group and I could still rank them all today." Along with rankings, hoods referred to each other as being a "right mad bastard," implying toughness, unpredictability, and dangerousness—valuable personal attributes that combine to distinguish a hood from his peers. However, with no hierarchical gang structure where the leaders get a cut of all of the profits of those lower down the ranks, very few of the hoods' exploits result in material or financial gain. Given that, in general, those with the highest status do not benefit materially, what are the payoffs to having high status? Those with a reputation for toughness are less likely to be picked upon in a fight, have more choice of sexual and criminal partners, and more opportunities to get involved in criminal activities. However, the main benefit is simply the knowledge that you are better or tougher than your peers.

2. The Behavior Displayed Is Closely Related to the Underlying Property Being Conveyed

The most obvious behavior that is associated with the property of toughness is violence; that is, both the ability and the willingness to use it. It has been argued that "violence is more functional to those who practice it in poor neighbourhoods than in middle-class ones, where self-control is valued and aggression is more likely to be channeled into business competition. Each group has its own culturally approved outlets for aggression."[10] The biographies of gangsters like the Kray twins and John McVicar all demonstrate that among certain groups and within particular social worlds violence is simply a fact of life.[11] While the hoods commit a range of violent acts, both expressive and instrumental, against people and property, fighting each other is pivotal in acquiring prestige and thereby determining status and rank. Verbal threats must be backed by a willingness to fight or else someone will soon see the bluff, and, among the hoods, there are significant gains to be made from these displays.[12]

Constantly instigating and winning fights is an obvious way of instilling fear in others and gaining a reputation for toughness: "You never ever turn down a fight—to get rank—the aim is to have people be scared of you" (Neil, ex-hood). However, the goal of these fights is not to kill or badly injure the opponent. Rather it is to identify who is the weaker party and get them to back down. The winner does not pursue the loser to injure him further or kill him, and when someone is badly injured it is because they failed to withdraw in time. These fights are physical contests of strength and have a direct impact on a hood's status.[13]

For the hoods, it is imperative that they be prepared to fight even if it is clear that they are they not going to win, and they may get badly injured. Violence-related status is primarily derived not from whether you win, but from your willingness to fight:

> No matter what, you'll fight anybody. Even if you are going to get slaughtered, you have to be up for it and even if you get a kicking you will still get status for being up for it. You never ever back down from a fight or else you'll go right down the pecking order and that is a heavier price than getting your head kicked in. (Pete, ex-hood)

In their study of the microsocial context of violent disputes among gang members in Chicago, Lorine A. Hughes and James F. Short report that a gang member's personal status could be elevated by fighting rival gang members "especially when the latter possessed some type of unfair advantage. Gang members who stood their ground in the face of unfavourable numerical odds gained prestige, for example, even in cases in which they had been defeated and in which the reputation of their gang may have suffered."[14]

Fighting someone who is much stronger is an example of a general principle in signaling theory: the 'full disclosure principle,' which states that "if some individuals stand to benefit by revealing a favourable value of some trait, others will be forced to disclose their less favourable values."[15] Therefore, if some hoods stand to benefit from fighting, others will be forced to fight as well; even though they will probably get beaten, it is better to fight and lose than not to fight.

Pete admitted to "standing crying in fear before a fight, but still fighting anyway." Only someone who is tough to the point of being uninterested or unable to calculate the cost would be able to overcome the fear and bear the physical pain. Those who chose not to fight are assumed to be weak. Because of the costs involved, fighting even when outclassed can be viewed as a reliable signal of strength and courage.

A signal's reliability depends upon the amount of investment it entails, and it makes logical sense to invest in signals that, although costly, are less costly than other actions that signal the same trait.[16] Verbal aggression and threats or "slabbering," as the hoods would say, is less costly than fighting. It does carry the risk of physical retaliation, and so signals recklessness and confidence, if not actual fighting ability:

> Slabberin' is directly related to power and violence. It's a tool that you'd use to maintain your status without having to go through the pain of violence, it's a way of gettin' people to back down, it's all an act, a game. I was a vicious bastard when it came to slabberin' at people. I could have you in tears right now if I wanted to. (Neil, ex-hood)

Research has indicated that adolescents who use drugs and alcohol are more likely to commit violent acts than those who do not abuse substances.[17] There is also a positive correlation between the severity and frequency of violent delinquency and the seriousness and frequency of drug taking.[18] Alcohol and drug use do not necessarily lead to violence, but in an environment where fighting is common, substances often act to encourage those inclined to be violent: "They [the hoods] would punch your head in for no reason if they're high or drunk. To an extent I'd be scared to walk past a lot of them" (Liam, age 21).

Joyriding, too, provides hoods with crucial information about one another. It is generally accepted in Western society that owning and driving fast cars is an attractive and exciting activity. Modern advertising and media images associate fast cars with status and often, for men, sexual prowess. Motor sports are watched by hundreds of thousands of people worldwide, and the racing drivers are applauded as heroic and daring figures, and they receive substantial financial rewards. It is therefore logical that owning and driving cars appeals to young men. We have also seen how stealing cars was "encouraged" by members of the paramilitary groups in the early days of the Troubles and grew popular among young people because of the risks and thrills involved.

When driving recklessly and at high speed, hoods endanger themselves and others. There is also the possibility that they might be chased and caught by either the IRA, the police, or the British army. These risks are further increased when hoods drive under the influence of alcohol and/or drugs. The mood-altering effect of the substances enhances the hedonistic "buzz" delivered by the cocktail of exhibitionism and danger. As the hoods speed wildly, executing hand-brake turns and ramming anything that gets in their way, so the feeling of exhilaration builds:

> I was blocked [drunk] all over Easter and got picked up [by the police] on the Andytown [Andersonstown] Road in a stolen car about three o'clock on Easter Monday. I was on my way over to a party in Botanic when the cops seen us and chased us and I got caught along with three wee birds [girls] 'cause I was too drunk to run. (Joe, age 18)

Even though using alcohol and drugs increases their chances of getting caught, their effect is to diminish any worries or concerns about the consequences of being caught. As the risks increase, the excitement intensifies: "[I]t's what puts the 'joy' in joyriding" (Angela, age 19).

A few hoods develop their careers instrumentally by selling stolen cars and car parts, but most just joyride. Those who drive the fastest cars and take the most risks are applauded, not least for their skills in stealing the cars in the first place. The joyriders persist because of the thrills involved, the influence from friends, and the desire to distinguish themselves as having the "best cars on the estate" (Sammy, age 18). Thus, joyriders steal powerful and expensive cars from the more affluent areas beyond West Belfast, because the car, when raced around the developments of West Belfast, acts as a "vehicle" for demonstrating the hoods' recklessness. Joyriding is thus costly in terms of time, investment, risk of capture, loss of income, risk of injury, and the loss of opportunity to engage in other financially rewarding criminal activities. These costs render it a more discriminating status-enhancing signal than much of the other behavior enacted by hoods and help to explain its popularity.

The hoods' drug and alcohol use is motivated by a mix of exhibitionism, defiance, and one-upmanship: "The primary reason I started usin' drugs was that I could tell my friends that I was takin' drugs and that was really cool," said Pete (ex-hood). As they get older, hoods are expected to graduate from solvents to drugs, such as marijuana and ecstasy. Some young people remain addicted to solvents and are still sniffing them at ages 17 and 18, leaving themselves open to ridicule from family and friends: "[M]y da' says stuff like 'look at you glue sniffin', gettin' on like a child'" (Ryan, age 14). Prolonged solvent use after the age that it is "socially acceptable" among hoods can be counteracted by extreme behavior in other areas. It is anti-status still to sniff glue at age 17, but it is very status-enhancing to be a prolific joyrider. Two of the most inexhaustible joyriders in the sample, Davy (age 17) and Paddy (age 19), were still sniffing glue. They compensated for their solvent use by their particularly reckless joyriding, and Davy claimed that using glue enhanced his joyriding: "When I take glue I just don't care and get into a car and away I'll go."

The IRA's uncompromising attitude toward drugs has given their use an additional air of adventure and excitement. Using drugs is bad, but drug dealing is an unambiguous act of defiance toward the IRA for which the punishment can be death: "They said I was dealin' [drugs] and put a gun to my head. The fella said he had an awful itchy finger and the next time he'd pull the trigger," said Fra (age 18). Most dealing among the hoods is at a very low level, no more than selling a small amount to friends, and stops as soon as the IRA begins to intervene. In the sample, only the most risk-prone persisted and expanded their business.

3. HOODS HAVE EFFECTIVE WAYS OF BROADCASTING THEIR BEHAVIORS

In order to communicate, a signal needs a receiver. Therefore, in order to act as a signal, others who understand the meaning of the behavior and who have an interest in acquiring information about the signaller must witness the action. Therefore we would expect hoods to have effective ways of broadcasting their exploits among their peers.

An overriding feature of joyriding is that it is a display activity only. Jack Katz notes that "[j]oyriding captures a form of auto theft in which getting away with something in celebratory style is more important than keeping anything or getting anywhere in particular."[19] Cars are therefore generally not stolen for economic gain, they are stolen and driven until they run out of fuel or are crashed and abandoned. Joyriders repeatedly return to the same locations to drive their cars, drawing large crowds of people out onto the streets to watch in horror or admiration. In Turf Lodge, when joyriders race up and down the Monagh Road, which runs through the middle of the development, large numbers of residents line the road on both sides, shouting and throwing stones, bricks and anything they can find at the cars racing by: "When people round here [Turf Lodge] go out on the streets they are armed to do some serious damage [to the joyriders]," says Local Resident T. In response, the joyriders turn their cars around and race back down the road, running the gauntlet underneath a hail of missiles. Occasionally the hoods will cover their faces with scarves and pull baseball hats down over the eyes, but generally they make little real attempt to hide their identity. The public nature of these displays increases the risks involved, and, crucially, it is a prime opportunity to impress other hoods; the more witnesses to their behavior, the better.

This desire for an audience was further exemplified when some hoods made a video of their joyriding "performance" and sold it in the playgrounds of local schools. The *Andersonstown News* reported that these videos show "a group of crazed joyriders tearing up and down the Monagh By-pass at terrifying speeds. At one point six stolen cars are on the road at the same time."[20] Other joyriders inside a stolen car parked at the side of the road filmed and then edited the video to conceal the identity of those in the film. However, the newspaper article notes that "faces can be seen and distinctive voices heard as they cheer each other on their journey of terror. The ringleader of the mob is repeatedly addressed as 'Rab.'"[21] "Rab's" reputation will have been enhanced considerably by this public acknowledgment of his unofficial leadership qualities. By filming their joyriding, the participants ensure that their "gamesmanship" and daring are witnessed and admired by as many young people as possible. The increased risk that the IRA and the police might identify them on the film only adds to their reputation for toughness.

Survey and ethnographic studies alike show that persistent property offenders spend much of their criminal gains on alcohol and other drugs.[22] Although not all hoods are persistent property offenders, their street lifestyle is hedonistic and typically includes the shared consumption of drugs and alcohol. Even when children as young as 9 or 10 start sniffing solvents, they do it in groups of two or three. These young people soon learn that by sniffing solvents they gain a reputation among their young friends for being tough, defiant, and rebellious. This behavior begins at an age when children particularly desire the esteem of their friends and associates, and are especially vulnerable to "peer pressure" and co-offending.[23] Tim (age 17) said, "I was taking [drugs] because I was a mad bastard. I wanted to try them and ended up liking 'em. I like the buzz and they're relaxing. I took them with me mates."

Shared drug use provides further evidence of the importance of displaying antisocial behavior. First, the audience confirms that drugs were indeed taken as claimed, and second, sharing drugs increases the social bond by locking the hoods together in mutual offending behavior. This is not just the sharing of a guilty secret, but the act requires that they must trust each other not to inform. In practice this means that if one member of the group informs, the others all have information about him or her that they can also pass on, thereby ensuring silence through their shared knowledge or, in other words, "I've got shit on you, you've got shit on me." This mutual blackmail creates low-quality trust among the group.[24]

The risk that accompanies sharing information of criminal activities is unavoidable if one has to advertise his or her exploits. Boasting about committing burglary does not provide enough information to bestow any kudos on the burglar because the audience cannot trust that the information is correct. Only the presence of stolen goods is proof enough that a burglary took place. In order for the burglary to be profitable the goods must be sold and the cooperation of other hoods is necessary for such transactions to take place. But this again increases the costs. There is the possibility that the stolen goods will fall into the hands of the IRA or the police, and that these items will be traced back to the burglar, or that another hood will inform. In light of the increased difficulties posed to would-be informants, hoods are forced to choose between protecting their friends by lying to the IRA and taking a harsh punishment, or giving information and getting a lesser sentence.

In West Belfast, sexual conquest operates as a signal among the male hoods, with the emphasis on having as many sexual partners as possible: "In many ways it was anti-status to have just one girlfriend or to be seen to be spending too much time with her. It was really frowned upon to stay in with your girl" (Neil, ex-hood). Wright and Decker also observed among their sample of burglars in St Louis, Missouri, that "[s]exual conquest was a much prized symbol of hipness through which the male subjects in our sample could accrue status among their peers on the street."[25]

The average age at which both the young men and women interviewed had their first sexual experience was 13. Despite being sexually active, hoods are reluctant to use contraception: just over one third reported that they used any. They assumed their female partners would take responsibility for contraception, and using condoms was considered "uncool." Research on contraception use has found that most individuals gain information about condoms at puberty and that this information chiefly comes from friends.[26] This suggests that attitudes toward condoms are formed early through peer interaction, and that modification after this time may be difficult. Given that using condoms is considered "uncool" by hoods, it is plausible that this attitude will affect the behavior of their peers and boys on their way to becoming hoods, who will not use condoms because they do not want to risk losing status. This is another indication of how these young people have become indifferent to the costs of their behavior, in this case the likelihood of contracting a sexually transmitted disease (STD), and pregnancy.

North and West Belfast have the highest levels of teenage mothers in Northern Ireland (the level is almost double the average in Northern Ireland), and, compared with other European countries, Northern Ireland has a high number of women under the age of twenty giving birth.[27] Thirteen of the male hoods in the sample had children and, with one exception, seemed unconcerned about their parental responsibilities. In all but one case, the relationship with their child's mother was over, and only two of the thirteen fathers intended to remain in contact with their partners and offspring. They gave no consideration to supporting their child in the future, and the child's existence merely served to signal that the hood had once had a sexual relationship with the mother.

An important feature of the hoods' behavior is their sexual competitiveness: "Girls were always a potential sign of weakness and people would deliberately set out to sleep with someone else's girlfriend and then you'd all start slabbering at the poor bastard "you're buying her chocolates while everyone else is riding her" (Pete, ex-hood). The primary intention may be to have sex, but the fact that it is then revealed rather than kept secret, as in bourgeois sexual infidelity, suggests that the hood's interest involves something more than that. Among the hoods, as explained by Neil, a former hood himself, the "nature of inter-personal relationships is to undermine other people's status, thereby increasing yours."

Punishment

Risky criminal and antisocial behavior acts as a signal for hoods seeking to communicate their toughness to other, less delinquent, young people. However, despite these attempts to differentiate, when communicating with other hoods, their signals are only semi-sorting because two problems remain. First, given that all hoods play these high-risk antisocial games, how can an individual hood distinguish himself further as the best competitor? After all, there are no gold medals to be won or league tables to publicly identify the members of the elite group. Second, hoods are known to be untrustworthy. In their desire for the esteem of other hoods, they frequently exaggerate the risks taken and the significance of their "achievements." The hoods are still faced with a primary trust dilemma: how do they know that the stories of offending as told by their peers are true? Furthermore, if they can't trust others' stories, how can they be sure that others will trust theirs? They expend considerable effort ensuring that they have effective ways of broadcasting their exploits, such as videotaping their activities and generally trying to maximize their audience. Another solution to this problem lies in a closer examination of the hoods' response to being policed and punished by the IRA and statutory criminal justice agencies.

Young offenders in West Belfast are subject to punishments from the statutory criminal justice system and the IRA. Both these agents base their practices on notions of deterrence: that criminal acts will be avoided because of fear of punishment.[28] In particular, with regard to PPAs, the hope is expressed that "beating and shooting will work for some" (Community Worker C), that is it will have a specific deterrent effect on young people who are in direct receipt of punishment.

Research on deterrence suggests that the certainty or likelihood of being caught and made liable to punishment has a substantially stronger deterrent effect than the severity of the punishment.[29] Yet, despite both the certainty and severity of punishment, the hoods persistently reoffend. Previous studies have reported that once the process of paramilitary intervention goes "beyond threats or warnings, the young people are likely to become involved in a cycle of reoffending, with a further escalation in the degree of punishment."[30] Both the statutory criminal justice agencies and the Republican Movement accept the limitations of their approaches. Commenting on the efforts of the Probation Board for Northern Ireland, former Chief Probation Officer Breidge Gadd noted that there is "a hard core of persistent offenders who in the mid-1990s defied all attempts to bring about change in their behaviour."[31] Sinn Féin agrees, and, over the past ten years, has repeatedly stated publicly that PPAs have not solved the problem of antisocial behavior.[32] Yet, the question still remains as to why the hoods persistently offend even after they have been punished and in the knowledge that there is a strong probability of more and increasingly severe punishment to come. As one former prisoner put it,

Most of these young people are on the run from the IRA and are on the run from the police, yet they are still doing what they are doing.

Why? Is it a lack of fear? . . . I began to realise that it certainly isn't a lack of fear, because they are hiding, they are running. If it wasn't fear you could do what you wanted to them. So what is it then? A lot of young people just accept that they'll get beaten or excluded from the area, just a resignation to their fate . . . for young people to accept that their fate is to have their legs broken or being shot . . . it's crazy. (Ex-prisoner F)

During the fieldwork in West Belfast, many community workers and local residents observed that hoods are proud of their punishment scars: "The first thing they think is that they'll get a claim and it becomes a set of stripes," notes Community Worker C. Another stated, "Some wear it like a medal and some it would stop them offending again. A lot don't care and want to actively oppose it and challenge it. They almost encourage it and invite it by their behavior. They have a 'you can't touch me' attitude" (Community Worker P). These comments raised the possibility that not only had punishment become destigmatized, but the hoods had commandeered the sanctions intended to control and restrict their behavior, and used them to gain prestige by integrating them into their signaling game.

Punishment as a Signal of Authenticity

All hoods engage in public displays of antisocial behavior and the more ostentatious these exhibitions are, the greater the amount of prestige. Among the hoods, notions of prestige, self-esteem, and the esteem of others are equated with non-ideologically motivated or mindless "toughness," which in turn is demonstrated by the extent to which the hoods offend and the risks that they are prepared to take. Hoods are, however, renowned for being untrustworthy and for exaggerating their exploits. The truth of what really happens is often hard to ascertain. In order to gain the esteem of others, hoods must be able to authenticate their claims to offending episodes.

Hoods tend not to offend alone, but in clusters of two or three, and large numbers of people often witness their joyriding. For the hoods, however, the evidence from eyewitness accounts of another's offending does not provide enough proof of authenticity. For example, a hood, person X, may boast that he stole a car from person Y, whose uncle, person Z, is a prominent member of the IRA. Other hoods may not be certain that person X ever committed that specific offense. Even if person X produces the car he allegedly stole, he may have bought the car from the real thief. If, however, person X is suddenly arrested for car theft and is sought after by person Z and other members of the IRA, then the chances increase dramatically that person X did indeed steal person Y's car.

Attracting the attention of the police, or more importantly the IRA, provides considerable evidence that the hood in question has committed an offense, and has a reputation for offending that goes beyond his small group. The only way in which this can be confirmed, however, is if at least one of these agents punishes the hood. Simply being interrogated and released without further action does not necessarily prove that the offense was committed and the hood got away with it. The only real proof is punishment, and the more severe the punishment, the more notable the offense and, consequently, the more exceptional the hood. For this reason, hoods will flaunt their offending, for example, goading the IRA by performing hand-brake turns in stolen cars outside homes of prominent members of the Republican Movement, or outside the Felons Club. In 1995, the IRA circulated a list, as noted earlier in this discussion, of accused drug dealers who were to be executed. This list was posted in pubs and on walls in West Belfast and as each drug dealer was killed, a tick appeared beside his name. Several hoods defiantly painted their own names alongside the posters thereby associating themselves with the "worst" people in the area and inviting the IRA to punish them, while at the same time signaling their own toughness to other hoods.

For the hoods, however, it is not simply a question of being punished. The agents of punishment, that is the state or the IRA, and the form that the punishment takes are also very important. The greatest sanction the state can impose is imprisonment, and to be imprisoned is a signal with an identifiable cost: loss of freedom and having to endure a prison regime. Neil (ex-hood) acknowledged these costs when he said, "The first time I got locked up I thought it was the end of the world. They put me away for three months and it felt like it was for the rest of my life." Yet, he continued, "by the second or third time I'd been inside, I couldn't care less about it." The specific deterrent effect of prison on those imprisoned diminished over time with each sentence. For example, Joe (age, 18) said, "It's wee buns in here [Hydebank YOC]. Anyway half of the estate is in. Mark and Colin came in the other day. Half of us are in here and half of us are under threat. YOC equals wee buns." The hoods may protest their innocence, but as Paddy (age, 19) put it, "If you can't do the time, don't do the crime."

For these young people imprisonment enhanced their belief that they possess the property of toughness as well as demonstrating it to others. Pete (ex-hood), for example, "was delighted when I was first put away at thirteen. I remember standing in the court thinking I must be a real gangster and it was just so cool." Imprisonment is, however, a less costly signal for the hoods than being caught and punished by the IRA: "I'd rather get lifted by the police, 'cause you're not going to get shot. There's always that fear with the IRA that you are going to get shot or kneecapped" (Liam, age 21). If we look again at the IRA's punishment tariff, and examine the hoods' responses to the various punishments, we can see how being punished by the paramilitaries acts as a signal among the hoods.

The hoods find exclusion by the IRA extremely difficult to endure. Being deprived of their own beds to sleep in, homes to live in, streets and housing developments to run about in, leaves hoods feeling isolated, frustrated, and anxious: "I wanna be able to walk down the street without having to look over my shoulder. I wanna be able to call down for my mate Frankie and go lookin' for good-looking girls" (Tim, age 17). Sammy (age 18) adds,

It's crap. Well, I can't walk about and do what I want. I used to go out for a drink and I can't do it no more. I used to just run about the estate, that's it. Just can't do the things I used to do. I would like to go about the estate without havin' to look over my shoulder all the time. The thing that really bothers me is not livin' in the house. [During one exclusion] I was living in a hostel and it was stinkin'. (Sammy, age 18)

Anger, bitterness, and a stubborn refusal to comply with the exclusion often accompany these feelings of isolation. Consequently, many hoods defy the exclusion and risk being physically punished by remaining in the area from which they have been excluded. This is preferable to living elsewhere until their exclusion is revoked or comes to a natural end. The hoods' refusal to comply with their sentence has been explained by their lack of personal, social, and life skills, which make it very difficult for them to develop or access new networks of support that would enable them to survive elsewhere.[33] Furthermore, if hoods no longer have access to their criminal network, they have limited opportunities to collaborate in order to make money and attain or maintain their position of power among the other hoods. They are a "nobody" in the areas to which they are exiled, and they have been deprived of the opportunity to communicate their toughness to their peers. They live in the knowledge that in West Belfast their absence means that they will be replaced in the hierarchy. It is thus preferable to stay and hide and risk attack than to live in obscurity elsewhere. For these same reasons hoods are also very reluctant to adhere to a curfew: "I was put on an eight o'clock curfew. I can't do what I want. I can't go out for drink; I can't go into the estate where my mates mess about but I go in anyway. Fuck them" (Tim, age 17). In order to maintain their status, hoods must stay in the game. The hoods' displays of toughness only have any real cachet if performed in front of other hoods in the specific West Belfast context where the signals are understood. Given the limited material benefits of the hoods' behavior, there is little to be gained in pursuing their antisocial activities outside the West Belfast area. By being prepared to live with the paramilitary threat and risk being physically punished, those hoods who stay are signaling their confidence in their cleverness, their powers of elusion, and their courage: "We just thought that we were better than them—especially the ones who gave us the kickings—they were just as thick as pig shit, all muscle no brains we thought we were just so fuckin' clever, outsmarting them all," according to Neil, an ex-hood. Given that the chances that a hood under paramilitary threat will be caught are high, their defiance in the face of the IRA's restrictions might seem crazy to the observer. However, infamy is better than anonymity, and, as a signal of toughness and authenticity, it is very discriminating.

Being "on the run" enhances a hood's prestige, but actually getting caught and punished by the IRA transports them into membership of an elite group:

> These young men seemed to consider the severity of their punishments and the urgency with which they were sought by the paramilitaries as proof of their personal significance. They used this and their experience of being shot as major elements in their presentation of self. They seemed to want to impress the listeners, and perhaps themselves, of their quick-witted and "cool" response to extreme danger and pain.[34]

Framing punishment by the IRA as a signal allows us to make sense of one of the most puzzling aspects of the hoods' behavior—that they turn up, by appointment, for their punishment. Given the prior knowledge of the imminent assault, why do they not abscond? Some do go on the run, but many appear on time, prepared to endure a violent attack that almost certainly will result in severe physical injuries. There have even been a number of reports of hoods queuing in line to receive "a bullet in the leg."[35] Often, hoods will have made preparations to endure the attack by getting drunk to dull the fear and pain. The explanation now appears simple: turning up, sometimes called "going for your tea" requires restraining every fearful urge to run away and therefore signals a heightened degree of toughness and courage to endure such physical pain. Running away, on the other hand, reveals panic and weakness. "Going for your tea" was a phrase used by the IRA to describe operations upon which members would embark that might result in imprisonment or death. By commandeering the expression, the hoods have allied punishment with daring and heroism.

The constraints imposed on the paramilitary groups since the 1994 by their political representatives and by the peace process have resulted in a decline in the number of shootings. Thus, even though the injuries that result from being shot are often less serious than those incurred from being beaten, the exceptionality of being kneecapped has made it the more discriminating signal. Danny (age 24) was excluded but had expected a physical punishment. He said, "If I had been shot I would have probably stopped. You know it's over in a couple of seconds, but if I'd got beaten and had them hold me down I'd have got worse in revenge." It seemed that, for Danny, being beaten also involved being humiliated, whereas being shot was somehow more honorable. Hoods who not only survive their punishment attack but also continue offending succeed in distinguishing themselves as being extremely tough. The fact that Bobby's wheelchair was found abandoned beside a stolen car several weeks after he was kneecapped was referred to as a measure of his toughness.

Many hoods proudly showed off their scars and happily rolled up their trouser legs to show off their misshapen and disfigured limbs: "You always wear your scars as symbols, something to be proud of," observed Pete, an ex-hood. The *Belfast Telegraph* newspaper carried a photograph of a young man whose right leg had been amputated following a punishment attack. On his left knee he displayed a tattoo with the words "Shoot Here."[36] In a similar manner, in Imperial Germany, facial scars left by saber dueling were highly prized as a sign of masculinity: "[I]n a 1912 session of the Reichstag, one deputy contended that hardly anyone achieved high state office who had not undergone the requisite facial."[37]

Pete recalled how he had been paid five pounds to shoot a friend in the leg with a blank-firing gun. The intention was to burn a hole in the knee to mimic being kneecapped. Pete was also paid to slice open the mimic's calf muscle with a razor blade. According to Pete, this was not an unusual occurrence: "You walk a very fine line and people often get their closest mates to give them a fat lip and a black eye so that it looks like they were done," he said. This was a 'win-win' situation for both Pete and the mimic. Pete was able to boast about inflicting such injuries: "I'd have done it for nothing or paid him to let me do it so I could tell people I'd done it and get status that way. It showed I was a mad, hard bastard." Likewise, even though the mimic was found out, his willingness to self-inflict these injuries acted as a signal. If he was tough enough to invite this pain and injury, then he would be tough enough to endure a punishment attack from a third party. Despite being exposed as a fraud, his actions still earned him respect. While this mimicking behavior may be marginal, it does provide further evidence that punishment was being used as a signal to communicate toughness.

For hoods in West Belfast, to be caught and physically punished by the

IRA and to then carry on offending is a reliable way of signaling status. PPAs inadvertently offered the hoods an opportunity to prove that their claims of toughness are true.

PUNISHMENT AS A SIGNAL OF LOYALTY

Being punished for antisocial behavior has another important function: it provides evidence of loyalty to one's friends. Weighing up another's trustworthiness and authenticating oneself as a trustworthy person is extremely problematic for the hoods. How can anyone prove that they are dependable and are not likely to inform under pressure? The hoods have, in part, solved this by electing to put their trustworthiness to an extreme test. When placed under immense pressure by the police and the IRA, eager for knowledge about other hoods, they must not inform. However, when panic and fear set in, information does get passed on. It is precisely because many have informed that the burden of proof lies with the detained hood to prove that he has not touted. The only reliable evidence he can provide of his trustworthiness is the punishment that he receives. Hoods assume that if the police do not charge someone, he got off lightly because he passed on information. This also follows when hoods go before the IRA. If anyone returns without being punished as expected—either unharmed, or without being excluded or curfewed—suspicion is aroused. Others wonder what deal was brokered for the detainee to have gotten away so easily, what information was passed on and who was it about?

Enduring harsh physical punishment as a signal of trustworthiness is extremely difficult, and during interrogation by the IRA, hoods may be torn between avoiding pain and not informing. Sean (age 17) had ignored the IRA's initial warning and had continued joyriding. He had been summoned by the IRA, and was expecting the worst. He was unsure whether to show up or not and turned to Paddy (age 19) for advice. Paddy recommended that Sean keep his appointment and outlined his dilemma:

> [F]irst, you don't want to be hurt. Second, you don't want to be seen as a "tout" [by your friends]. . . . Thirdly, you don't want to be seen as

a tout by the IRA. Fourthly, how can you get away with just being hurt a little bit? . . . Fifth, you don't know if you give over some information to the IRA if they will let you off lightly because you've helped them or make it a worse sentence because they hate touts themselves, and although they may have got some more information you've just shown yourself as the scum of the earth. [Six], if you don't give the IRA any information, you might get away lightly because you might be a hood but you're not a tout or they might make it worse because you've not cooperated.

The problem of passing on information is further complicated because the hoods cannot be sure where the IRA's values lie on the issue, and therefore do not know which strategy—refusal to cooperate or compliance—is optimal.

In addition to the dilemma of how to respond when under interrogation, hoods also have to balance the number of times that they manage not to get punished versus having to take the full consequences. "Getting away with it" provides evidence of a certain prowess and cleverness, but if it happens too often they may come under suspicion. Tim's sentence was to be shot in both ankles. However, the gun jammed after it was fired at just one of his ankles. This incident sent a double signal. Tim was "hard" and "bad" enough to be shot, but the fact that he got a chance reprieve and one of his ankles was saved, signaled both luck and cunning—both attributes admired by the hoods.

The hoods' criminal and antisocial behavior can be seen as a set of delinquent practices that, taken together, form a competition for prestige among the hoods. This chapter has argued that the conditions also exist for these behaviors to be viewed as a costly signaling game that produces a semi-sorting equilibrium. Furthermore, PPAs help to establish a hood's status by authenticating his offending behavior, testing his toughness and courage, and providing evidence of his loyalty to other hoods.

FIVE

Loyalists

So far, this book has addressed extralegal policing and punishment in Catholic West Belfast only. In this chapter I make some general observations about informal policing and justice and patterns of offending in Loyalist areas, and these comparisons will be used to shed more light on the situation in West Belfast. In particular, this chapter aims to show how a difference in the goals and structure between the Loyalist paramilitary organizations and those of the IRA affects these organizations recruitment strategies. This in turn influences the actions of young people disposed to risk taking and antisocial behaviors.

There are many similarities between the Nationalist/Republican and Unionist/Loyalist working-class communities in Belfast; they share problems of high unemployment, poverty, and crime. These similarities become very apparent if we compare the bordering areas of Falls/Clonard, whose population is 95.1 percent Catholic, and Greater Shankill, whose population is 91.5 percent Protestant. The percentage long-term unemployment rate in both areas is almost twice that of the rate in Northern Ireland, and in 2007 over half of all those between the ages of 16 and 74 had no educational qualifications, as compared with 41.6 percent in the general population in Northern Ireland.[1] Comparing the two types of communities, Robert McLiam Wilson writes, "Both types of places were simply deep cores of poverty. They could paint their walls any colour they wanted, they could fly a hundred flags and they still wouldn't pay the rent."[2]

While the IRA dominates Republican paramilitarism, the Protestant community has a much more fragmented paramilitary landscape. There are two main Loyalist paramilitary groups. The larger of the two, the Ulster Defence Association (UDA), was formed in September 1971. It was not declared illegal until 1992, and from 1973, it used the cover name of Ulster Freedom Fighters (UFF) to claim responsibility for killing Catholics.[3] Together, the UDA and UFF have been responsible for 259 deaths, 71 percent of whom were Catholic, between 1969 and 2001.[4] Many of the attacks carried out by the UDA are aimed at intimidating Catholics.[5] The UDA is organized into six brigades, each under the command of a "brigadier," with battalions, companies, platoons, and sections. Their steering committee, the Inner Council, is composed of brigadiers from each of the areas plus occasionally some paramilitary or political advisors. The brigadiers exercise a great deal of autonomy outside of the control of the Inner Council.

The Ulster Volunteer Force (UVF) was founded in 1966, was declared illegal in 1974, is smaller in number than the UDA, but is much deadlier.[6] It is linked to the Red Hand Commandos (RHC).[7] Despite its policy of no first strikes against Catholics, between 1969 and 2010, the UVF killed 433 people, 64 percent of whom were Catholic.[8] The UVF has a more centralized command structure and operates under a single commanding officer. Its decision-making is more coherent than that of the UDA, and it exerts stronger control over its wider membership.

The UDA and UVF may share the same ideology and use similar methods, but they are uneasy bedfellows. They allied in 1991 under the umbrella of the Combined Loyalist Military Command (CLMC) to negotiate the cease-fires, but this coalition collapsed acrimoniously in 1997. Both groups compete for the allegiance of working-class Protestants and the spoils of conflict. They both have ready access to weapons and a supply of manpower willing to use violence.

One consequence of the lack of coherency and discipline, particularly within the UDA, has been that minor disputes and fracas have escalated very quickly into all out violence.[9] In March 1975 the first significant feud occurred. Members from both the UDA and UVF were shot and their homes attacked by petrol bombs. Since then feuds have erupted periodically between these groups. In August 2000 the dispute between the UDA and UVF on the Shankill Road, over drug dealing and territorial control, resulted in seven deaths and over 281 families seeking rehousing because of intimidation.[10] It has been claimed that this feud "caused more damage to the social infrastructure of the area than what the Republicans had managed to inflict throughout the Troubles."[11] The UDA's looser organization undoubtedly contributed to the larger number of internal feuds between rival factions of the organization, such as the one that occurred on the Shankill Road in 2002–2003. Eight people died in this feud, and sixty others, including Johnny "Mad Dog" Adair and his family, fled Northern Ireland for England and Scotland.[12]

Paramilitary Punishment Attacks (PPAs)

The first Loyalist punishment shootings were recorded alongside those of Republicans in 1973. The police did not begin to record beatings until 1988, and they do not record which organization was responsible for each attack. However, it is assumed that the larger organizations, the UDA and the UVF, are responsible for the bulk of the attacks and unless stated explicitly the two organizations are considered together. Official statistics use the broad categories of punishment shooting and punishment assault to describe this type of Republican and Loyalist paramilitary activity, and it is tempting to think that the phenomena are the same in both communities. Loyalists are simply mimicking Republican behavior. One problem is that less is known about the reasons for incidences of Loyalist PPAs than those carried out by the IRA. Unlike the IRA, the Loyalists rarely issue statements explaining their actions and apparently feel less compelled to justify their behavior to their host communities. The evidence presented in this chapter suggests, however, that PPAs perpetrated by the Loyalists are not part of a wider strategy to usurp or discredit the state but are due to feuds among Loyalist groups, discipline within organizations, and the settling of scores between individuals over issues related to criminal activity such as drugs and the control of territory.

In chapter 1, I argued that PPAs in Republican areas are a result of the interaction between the demand from the local population and the supply of this service by the IRA. The demand is driven by the many costs to ordinary nationalists and Republicans of using the statutory criminal justice system. These costs include a belief in the lack of efficacy and efficiency of the police and the courts, a deep-seated fear and mistrust of the police, and fear of reprisals from neighbors and the IRA, who view any contact with the police as evidence of collusion. The supply side was driven by strong incentives within Sinn Féin and the IRA to exclude the police from their territory to enable them to 1) carry out their activities undisturbed, 2) bolster support for their wider political cause by providing retribution to victims of crime, and 3) signal their monopoly of the use of violence, and thus their power and control within their territory. Furthermore, they had a ready supply of manpower willing to use violence. This same combination of conditions does not exist within Loyalist communities, yet the rate of PPAs has remained high, and from 1997 it consistently exceeded those perpetrated by Republicans.

The Demand for PPAs

Steve Bruce argues that as traditional supporters of the union between Great Britain and Northern Ireland, "[t]he Loyalist population do not feel the need to create a range of institutions outside or against those of the state."[13] There are several components that help to explain this lack of demand, with specific reference to policing and justice.

The demand for policing and punishment from the IRA can be traced to the late 1960s and early 1970s. During this period, working-class Protestants living in interface areas also suffered a great deal. However, the Protestant community as a whole did not experience the same intensity of violence in the form of riots and clashes between the army and police as their Catholic counterparts; nor were they subject to internment. The North Belfast postal district of BT14 is the most religiously mixed district of the city and has experienced the highest intensity of violence and here 7 percent of Protestant deaths were perpetrated by the security forces as compared to 24 percent of Catholic deaths.[14] Throughout the Troubles, Catholics experienced higher levels of violence (both direct and indirect) than Protestants, were twice as likely to have been intimidated, and were about one third more likely to have been a victim of a violent incident.[15]

The police, the army, and the Ulster Defence Regiment (UDR)[16] presented the IRA with a range of targets in their fight, and, by attacking the police and the UDR, the IRA were, in effect, attacking Protestants. In total 1,288 Protestants were killed in the Troubles between 1969 and 2001. Of these 76 percent (981) were killed by Republican paramilitaries, 18 percent (234) by Loyalist paramilitaries, and 3 percent (43) by British security forces.[17] Whereas direct personal experience of violence increased sympathies for Republican groups among Catholics, it decreased sympathies for the Loyalist paramilitary groups among Protestants. While Catholics looked to Republican paramilitaries for retaliation, Protestants continually turned to the security forces for redress.[18]

Nonetheless, in the early 1970s Protestants felt the need to establish vigilante groups like the Shankill Defence Association, which boasted 2,000 members.[19] These groups patrolled Protestant neighborhoods and claimed to offer protection if the police and army could or would not. While the Republican CCDC's vigilance was against Loyalists and the security forces, the Loyalist groups were mainly on the lookout for Republicans. For a brief period during this time barricades were set up in Loyalist areas and, intensely irritated by the existence of no-go zones in Republican neighborhoods, the UDA created no-go zones for the police and army in 1972. These did not last long, and their purpose was more symbolic than defensive; they would be removed when the British army moved into the Republican no-go zones. Community development projects emerged on the Shankill Road and in other Protestant enclaves like the Taughmonagh estate in South Belfast. These groups battled the state over housing, health and leisure facilities, public transport, and the like. But, while residents on the Falls Road had a long tradition of opposition to the state and readily linked community affairs and national politics, working-class Protestants were much less inclined to make these connections.[20] In order to help their community, Catholics were willing to work outside of the law and not use statutory agencies, which they considered to be often discriminatory. The Protestant self-image was more law-abiding. This difference is illustrated clearly in the development of community restorative justice schemes in Loyalist and Republican areas. Northern Ireland Alternatives was established in the Protestant Shankill area in 1996 and has programs in three other Protestant areas in Northern Ireland.[21] From the outset it adopted a partnership approach with the statutory criminal justice system, receiving referrals from the police, probation and social services, and the courts. Community Restorative Justice Ireland (CRJI) was established in 1999 in Catholic West Belfast, and outside of Belfast it has programs in two other Catholic areas in Northern Ireland.[22] In giving evidence to the Northern Ireland Affairs Committee

on Community Restorative Justice, Jim Auld, Director of CRJI, emphasized the misgivings with the police held by members of the communities with whom CRJI worked. Rather than communicate directly with
the police, CRJI used the probation or social services as intermediaries
referring cases involving children or allegations of sexual abuse to them
on the understanding that these agencies would then contact the police.[23]

Events such as the Anglo-Irish Agreement in 1985 and the policing
of Orange parades throughout the late 1990s brought Loyalists and police into direct conflict reminiscent of clashes between Republicans and
the police. Protestors threw fireworks, petrol bombs, and blast bombs at
the police, who retaliated with plastic bullets.[24] Injuries were sustained,
tensions rose, and relations were damaged between Catholics and Protestants and between Protestants and the police. The police's muscular
response at parades was not accompanied by a draconian crackdown on
the Protestant population more generally, and so these events did not en-
gender the same amount of bitter resentment among Protestants against
the security forces as the ongoing conflict has stirred up among Catholics.

Evidence from the British Social Attitudes Survey showed that Protestants are generally much more satisfied with the police than Catholics,
but for members of both religions, levels of satisfaction with the police
decline with social class.[25] Some Loyalists involved in criminal activity
may have reason to dislike the police and even obstruct their investigations, but they do not question the fundamental legitimacy of the criminal justice agencies in the way that Republicans do. There is a strong
sense within working-class Protestantism that "at the end of the day" the
police and the security forces are "theirs."[26]

This sense of ownership is a reflection of the religious composition of
the police. Prior to the Patten reforms implemented in the Police (Northern Ireland) Act 2000, less than 10 percent of the police force were Catholic. The act legislated that in appointing trainee police officers, the Chief
Constable should appoint, from a pool of qualified applicants, an even
number of persons one half of whom are from a Catholic community
background and one half who are not. Figures for April 1, 2006, showed
that 19 percent of the regular police service is from the Catholic community, compared to 8 percent in November 2001.[27] Data on the distribution of social class within the police is unavailable, but the fact that

they recruit from the same broad community increases the police's informational advantage. Bruce recounts the story of a police constable whose Protestant girlfriend told him that her brother had been the driver of the gang who had murdered Jack Kielty, a Catholic businessman, in 1988. The policeman reported this information and his girlfriend's brother and three others involved in the killing were arrested and subsequently convicted.[28]

Loyalist paramilitaries take fewer risks than Republicans when carrying out PPAs. Republicans are more likely to attack a larger number of victims in any one incident and to carry out their attacks in public places, thereby increasing the number of potential witnesses to the assault. Yet, Loyalists are four times more likely to be convicted of PPA-related offenses as Republicans.[29] Like their Catholic counterparts, many Protestant victims of PPAs may have criminal records but they do not share the same underlying fear of the police. They may be reluctant to give evidence about the assault against them, but they are more willing to do so than Catholic victims. This is also true of Protestant witnesses, who have not faced the social ostracism or the direct punishment associated with allegations of cooperating with the police as have Catholics in Republican areas. The average clear-up rate of recorded crime in mostly Protestant East Belfast for the period 2004 to 2006 was 28 percent and in West Belfast it was 22 percent.[30] Neither figure is very large, but the greater cooperation with the Protestant community increases the police's ability to gather information and thus be more effective in clearing up crime in Protestant areas. I will return to the amount and type of crime in Loyalist areas toward the end of this chapter.

Differences in support for Loyalist and Republican paramilitary activity can be seen very clearly in the various fortunes of the political representatives of the two types of paramilitarism. Sinn Féin has dominated the Catholic working-class vote since 1997, and in the 2005 Westminster elections the party overtook the more moderate Social Democratic and Labour Party (SDLP) to become the largest nationalist political party.[31] Support for all aspects of the IRA's campaign may be ambiguous, but Sinn Féin's electoral success is a clear public endorsement of the Republican project. In stark contrast, the Progressive Unionist Party (PUP), representing the UVF, and the Ulster Democratic Party (UDP), representing the UDA, have failed to garner any significant support. They face greater competition for the working-class Protestant vote in that they compete not only against each other but also the Ulster Unionist Party (UUP) and, more formidably, Ian Paisley's Democratic Unionist Party (DUP). The UDP dissolved in 2001, and the PUP managed to gain only 1 percent of the share of the vote, or one seat, in the 2003 Northern Ireland Assembly Elections.[32] Their leader, David Ervine, had been a senior UVF figure who had served a ten-year prison sentence for explosive-related offenses. He had credibility within the paramilitary constituency and gained wide respect among the political classes. The journalist David McKittrick described Ervine as being "one of the most interesting and unexpected figures of the Northern Ireland [T]roubles, emerging from a violent organization to become an advocate of peace and politics."[33] His untimely death in 2007 left a hiatus within the PUP, and its future looks uncertain. Despite David Ervine's best efforts, the PUP could not find a clear and unique political message and, unlike Sinn Féin's association with the IRA, the PUP's links to the UVF made it less rather than more attractive to voters.

Working-class Protestants may be better disposed toward the police than Catholics, but they have reported frustration with the leniency of the police in dealing with ordinary crime, noting that the police prefer to concentrate their efforts on politically motivated crime.[34] For their part, the police complain about the lack of "overt support" when it comes to providing the kind of hard evidence that allows them to make convictions.[35] Nonetheless, the better relationship between the police and Protestants points to less of a demand for PPAs and raises the puzzle as to why the rate of PPAs by Loyalists has increased in recent years, overtaking that of PPAs perpetrated by Republicans? The answer to this puzzle lies in a detailed analysis of those who are responsible for these attacks.

SUPPLY OF PPAS

Like Republicans, Loyalist paramilitary groups have been carrying out PPAs since the beginning of the Troubles. As figure 2 illustrates, between 1973 and 1985, they were responsible for significantly less punishment shootings than Republicans. This reflects both the low demand for non-

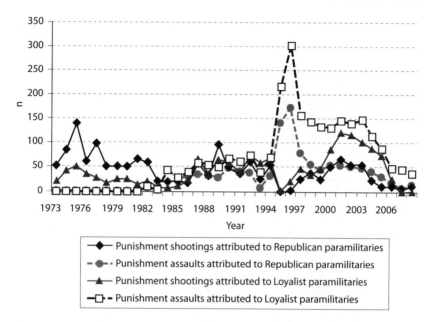

Figure 2 Paramilitary punishment shootings and assaults attributed to Republican and Loyalist paramilitary groups 1973–2008. *Source*: Author's compilation from PSNI 2003, 2009. Punishment assaults are included from 1982 onward.

state policing among the Protestant working-class population and a disinterest among Loyalist paramilitaries in taking on a policing role. The UVF's view was that "law and order was about keeping a close watch on Catholics, for the protection of Protestants" rather than surveillance of, and intervention with, Protestants.[36] As pro-state terrorists, Loyalists believed their role was to augment state forces which, in their view, were often too lenient in fighting Republicans.

Between 1983 and 1997 the number of PPAs perpetrated by Loyalists more closely mirrored that of PPAs by Republicans. Relations between the police and the working-class Protestant community worsened during this time. Sammy Duddy, a representative of the Ulster Political Research Group (UPRG), which advises the UDA on political matters, argues, "Years ago we used to take those we had known to have offended to the police, but they were just asked to become informers so that had to be stopped. That's why punishment shootings started."[37] Like the IRA, the UDA had concerns about its internal security and established a "Special

Assignments Section" dedicated to uncovering informers. At the same time, the growing evidence on collusion between the police and Loyalists shows that their relationship was not as straightforwardly antagonistic as that between Republicans and the police.[38] The key point is that the same strong incentives to keep the police and security forces away from their host population did not exist.[39]

The cease-fire issued by the Combined Loyalist Military Command (CLMC) in 1994 resulted in a dramatic reduction in shootings and an increase in assaults. For example, in 1995 there were only three shootings but seventy-six assaults carried out by Loyalists. The effect of the cease-fire was short lived, and 1996 saw an increase in recorded attacks, the highest number of them up until that year. When Republican attacks dropped off in 1997, Loyalists continued undeterred by the peace process, and since then their numbers have continuously surpassed those of Republicans. Loyalists have been less engaged in the political process and have not felt so restricted by the "no shooting" prerequisite of a cease-fire. The UVF has always maintained more discipline over its membership than the UDA, but both groups are less internally coherent than the IRA, which suggests that even if their leadership called for a restriction on the use of guns, this order would be difficult to enforce. Although there are no accurate figures on exiling, the Independent Monitoring Commission (IMC) noted in their Fifth Report that the numbers of individuals being exiled are roughly evenly split between Loyalists and Republicans.[40]

One effect of there being several groups that operate simultaneously but not cooperatively is that Loyalist paramilitary activity has a more haphazard and volatile feel.[41] This is enhanced by their unpredictability and cruelty in selecting and killing their victims. All too often, a foiled attack on their intended victim has resulted in the death of an innocent Catholic who happened to be in the wrong place at the wrong time. Loyalist hit squads do not like to return home without a "kill," and there have emerged chilling stories of torturing victims in Loyalist "romper" rooms.[42] It is therefore reasonable to surmise that the Loyalist approach to PPAs would be more indiscriminate than that of the better-disciplined and monopolistic IRA. The UVF's "Social Units" appear to be the closest thing that either Loyalist group has had to the IRA's civil administration. The evidence of systematic activity by these units is thin. The UVF claimed, for a time, to operate a proportional tariff. In 1996 newspapers reported that a "court" had been established in a pub on the Shankill Road. This court was issuing a system of fines whereby joyriding incurred a £150 penalty, theft a £500 fine, and drug dealing up to £1,000. It is more likely that this tariff reflected the UVF's assessment of an individual's ability to pay rather than any sense of the penalty being proportional to the seriousness of the crime. Drug dealing is much more lucrative than joyriding.[43] The UVF has also been accused of fining members who left voluntarily or were expelled. One former UVF commander was told to pay £30,000 to guarantee his future safety, and another former member, accused of drug dealing, was fined £50,000 in return for permission to live safely in Northern Ireland.[44] Again, these figures say more about their earnings than about the seriousness with which the UVF views their defection. The UVF clearly expects that people such as former commanders are able to pay.

Other nonviolent methods of punishing members of Loyalist communities have been explored by the paramilitaries. In March 2003, the North Belfast brigade of the UDA announced a nonviolent policy of "naming and shaming" to replace beatings and shootings. Two young men accused of theft were forced to stand on the side of a busy main road for three hours with placards reading, "We are scum who robbed our own people."[45] This policy was short-lived and was not adopted by the organization more widely.

Andrew Silke and Max Taylor's comparison of the age profile of Republican and Loyalist PPAs shows that while the vast majority of victims are under 30 years of age, Loyalist victims still tend to be older than IRA victims. Forty-three percent of IRA victims are under 20 as compared to 26 percent of Loyalist victims; and 26 percent of Loyalist victims are between the ages of 30 and 39, whereas only 12 percent of IRA victims are in this age bracket.[46] Olwen Lyner, Chief Executive for the Northern Ireland Association for the Care and Resettlement of Offenders (NIACRO), who host the Base 2 project, which works with people under paramilitary threat, has noted that members of the younger age group are more likely to be threatened because of antisocial behavior such as petty theft and vandalism, and threats to the older age group are more often prompted by drug-related issues, feuds, and internal discipline.[47] This evidence supports the IRA's claims of attempts to tackle juvenile delinquency and crime but weakens similar statements made by Loyalists. The older age profile of Loyalist victims suggests that internal disciplinary issues and feuds more often prompt their PPAs. An ill-disciplined culture leads to an increase in infringements requiring punishment and a need to use violence to discipline and control members.

Loyalist PPAs peaked between 2001 and 2005, correlating with an increase in feud-related violence. Throughout most of the Troubles, the Loyalists had an uneasy union against their common enemy: Republicans. As the IRA cease-fire has held, so the Loyalists have turned inward. For example, during a ten-day period in October 2003 four men, ages 43, 45, 39 and 29, were shot in both legs in a Loyalist area of North Belfast. The shootings were linked to a failed take-over bid of the leadership of the North Belfast UDA.[48] A year earlier Davy Mahood, a senior spokesman for the UPRG, was shot in both legs following a four-month investigation by the UDA. He was accused of treason.[49] Successive IMC reports have accused the UDA, UVF, and Loyalist Volunteer Force (LVF) of dealing drugs, extortion, robbery, and the sale of counterfeit goods.[50] Retribution for personal slights and competition over these illegal markets have all contributed to the numbers of PPAs. In contrast the number of PPAs fell between 2006 and 2008, which was also a period of relative quiet and reflection within Loyalism. Also during this period, both the UDA and UVF developed new codes of conduct covering members' behavior with the expectation that this would lead to a reduction in violence.[51]

Younger victims are more likely to have fallen foul of the Loyalist paramilitaries because their local brigade did not sanction their antisocial behavior. In June 2002, Johny "Mad Dog" Adair's teenage son Jonathan was beaten with baseball bats and iron bars as punishment for a robbery of an 84-year old pensioner. In August 2002, he was shot in both legs for cumulative antisocial misdemeanors. These incidents serve to illustrate the difficulty in attributing responsibility for attacks. There have been claims that both the beating and the shooting were carried out with Adair senior's permission.[52] If true, this adds a particular perversity to these assaults and acts as strong signal of Adair's territorial control and ruthlessness at that time. However, John White a close family friend and associate stated that Adair might not have known or sanctioned either of the attacks, adding "Issues like this can be dealt with at a local level and do not always go through the hierarchy of the organization."[53] This statement resonates with the decentralized structure of the UDA, but it was also made at a time when Adair was considering standing for office in local elections and wanted to briefly distance himself from violence.

Crime and Antisocial Behavior

The staunchly Protestant and Loyalist Shankill area of West Belfast is separated from Catholic West Belfast by the peace-line—a wall that has been erected to keep the two communities apart, but can be crossed at several points. The two areas are only one or two streets apart. Despite being so geographically close to the dramatic sights and sounds of joyriding, in general, young people in Loyalist areas do not joyride. The Northern Ireland Office recorded that 88 percent of those released from prison, convicted of Taking and Driving Away (TDA) between 1995 and 1997, were Catholic.[54] Therefore, while Loyalist young offenders might on occasion steal a car for parts or to sell on, they will not drive around in it publicly flaunting their offense in front of residents and paramilitaries. Nor does there appear to be the same clearly defined group of hoods. There are a number of reasons for these differences.

In West Belfast paramilitary power is concentrated among members of the IRA and those strongly associated with the organization; they have achieved a monopoly. As we have seen in chapter 3, entry into the IRA is restricted and hoods were not viewed as being trustworthy and reliable enough to become members. This exclusion severely constrained the opportunities for the hoods to achieve community recognition, and compelled them to concentrate on attaining and maintaining respect among other hoods, as well as on achieving a villainous reputation with the wider community—infamy is better than obscurity, hence the very public displays of joyriding.

Within the Loyalist communities, there is greater diversity within paramilitarism and "pseudo-paramilitarism," ranging from groups that are very politically motivated and committed to their political cause, to those that are simply a forum for petty criminality. One former offender, at age 16, stole an arms cache from a Loyalist paramilitary group and created DUST (Defenders of Ulster Shotgun Team). (The name was chosen because of the easy acronym.) Their primary activity was to sit in a garage drinking and admiring their loot. As a group, they did not survive being raided by the police. As individuals, they barely survived the wrath of their paramilitary victims!

All of the credible Loyalist armed groups hold some power in their strongholds and are feared because of their potential recourse to violence. Not only do the UDA and the UVF have less strict recruitment criteria than the IRA, but also there is evidence of both organizations engaging in recruitment drives from the mid-1990s onward in an effort to bolster their youth wings in the wake of an increase in internecine feuding.[55] It is therefore easier for young people involved in petty crime to be absorbed into an organization and derive some prestige from that membership. (Some, like the members of DUST, do not join a bona fide armed group, but the proportion of these nonaligned young people is smaller than that in Republican areas.) These new recruits remain delinquent but their criminal activities may change or escalate to selling drugs, contraband cigarettes, and alcohol on behalf of their armed group. A community worker who works with both Loyalist and Republican young people noted, "In East Belfast your average young person is different. It is more petty crime and not so persistent and consistent." However, it is perhaps the case that their offending may be just as persistent but is less visible because much of it takes place under the umbrella of activities of the paramilitary groups. PPAs against this type of young person are carried out more often because they have unpaid debts or have not been sufficiently cooperative with their local brigade. There have also been reports that young people who resist recruitment may be assaulted.

Loyalist paramilitarism thus performs a similar function to that of youth gangs in the United Kingdom and the United States. It provides a forum in which status can be gained through advancement up the para-military hierarchy, and PPAs act more to enforce norms of cooperation than they do to usurp formal policing or provide marginalized youth with a perverse signal of toughness. Differences in the structure of the UDA, UVF, and the IRA are also important. The IRA's more centralized and disciplined command structure and arguably more tightly focused ideology and actions have meant that promotion has been closely linked with military skill and courage. The federal structure of the UDA and UVF, where brigades act more autonomously of the central command, gives more opportunity to become a "big fish in a small pool" to a larger number of people. Advancement is not limited to military prowess but may also be associated with profit-making ability from criminality and therefore widens the pool of potential members.

Republican and Loyalist armed groups use very similar methods in car-rying out PPAs, but these obvious similarities belie important analytical distinctions in understanding the behavior in the two communities. In particular, among Protestants the supply of PPAs appears to outweigh the demand from the community. The better relationship between working-class Protestants and the state means that the costs of turning to the police for retribution and redress against ordinary crime are con-siderably lower than in the Catholic community. And we have seen that PPAs are much less exclusively directed toward delinquent young people than is the case with Republican PPAs. Young Protestants are as likely to receive a PPA for not cooperating with the local brigade as they are for acts of delinquency against local people. Furthermore, a significant proportion of PPAs are related to internal disciplinary issues, business deals gone sour, and feuds and turf wars between members of the main Loyalist groups.

The structure of paramilitarism in working-class Protestant commu-nities—a larger number of groups, more relaxed entry requirements, less internal discipline—has resulted in differences in the types of delinquent behavior that can be observed in the two communities. Specifically, the fact that Protestant young people have not developed the same joyriding culture as Catholic young people is directly related to these structural differences. Protestant young people do signal their toughness through criminal prowess, but their absorption into paramiltiarism means that the signaling game is more likely to occur within the ranks of a hierarchal paramilitary organization. They do not need to gain notoriety among each other through the very public display of joyriding.

CONCLUSION

This book has sought to provide a detailed account of nonstatutory crime control in Belfast and, in particular, the prevalence of PPAs in Republican and Loyalist controlled neighborhoods. The over 5,000 recorded shootings and beatings and countless warnings, exiles, and curfews have been a violent and terrifying sideshow to the 3,560 deaths attributed directly to the political Troubles between 1969 and 2006–2007. Their existence provided the watching world with yet more evidence for the barbarism and seeming irrationality of the conflict in Northern Ireland, and, despite the frequent condemnations by politicians from both sides of the political divide, the attacks have continued.

In Republican areas, the conditions of a demand for policing and the presence of a willing and capable supplier, who from the very early days of the Troubles monopolized the use of violence, have been present. The eruption of political violence in the 1970s and the consequent deterioration of relations between the police and the local population increased the costs to residents of using the statutory system and created the demand for nonstate policing. This demand was met and fostered by the IRA, whose interest in supplying policing has been a complex mixture of self-interest in encouraging dependence and loyalty among the local population and a genuine desire by some in the movement to provide a service to the community. These conditions have sustained the informal system over the years.

The power-sharing agreement between the DUP and Sinn Féin, which facilitated the resumption of the devolved parliament in June 2007, has ushered in a new phase in Northern Ireland's political history. At a special Ard Fheis held on January 28, 2007, Sinn Féin, with the support of the membership of the IRA, decided to support state policing and the criminal justice system. This very significant change in Republican policy should remove many of the costs of reporting crime to the statutory criminal justice system. Residents should no longer fear intimidation or loss of reputation if they contact the police and, in turn, the police ought to be able to investigate crimes more effectively and efficiently. Furthermore, as part of their new commitment to policing and justice, the leadership of the IRA will no longer be willing to supply people to carry out these violent acts.

In Loyalist areas the situation regarding PPAs has been somewhat different from the Republican case. The costs to residents of using the statutory criminal justice system have been lower, and thus there has been less demand from the local community that the paramilitaries take on a policing role. Although the methods used are similar to those of the IRA, the variation in age of victims strongly suggests that PPAs are being used not only to control and punish young delinquents but also to instill discipline and settle scores both within and between the UDA and the UVF. The adoption of new codes of conduct combined with the UVF's statement in May 2007, in which it declared that the "Ulster Volunteer Force and Red Hand Commando will assume a nonmilitary, civilianised role," are signals of an intention within Loyalist paramilitarism to reduce levels of violence. The statement also encouraged members to support restorative justice projects in order to tackle criminality and antisocial behavior. The UVF, however, has not committed to decommissioning its weapons, and so Loyalist intentions to reduce the amount of violence should be viewed with caution.

A key condition for the continued involvement of both Republican and Loyalist armed groups in policing and punishment has been the supply of manpower skilled in, and willing to carry out, violent PPAs. If, as a result of the decreased costs of using the statutory system, demand lessens, how will the individual perpetrators of PPAs respond? They could simply no longer use these skills or it is likely that some will redeploy them elsewhere. The IMC reports that members of the INLA, Continuity IRA, Real IRA, LVF, UDA, and the UVF are involved in drug dealing, extortion, fuel and cigarette smuggling, money laundering, and robbery, and the extent to which proceeds from these activities are for individual gain only or go to the respective organizations remains ambiguous.[1] Members of the IRA are also involved in tax fraud, smuggling, and money laundering, although the IMC emphasizes that the IRA leadership has stated explicitly that their members should not be involved in criminal activity and the organization should not profit from criminality. Gambetta argues that in Northern Ireland organized crime activity "stems simply from an economy of scale . . . from the low additional cost incurred in expanding the use of violence from one context (politico-religious) war to another (racketeering)."[2] In both Republican and Loyalist areas, the organizational infrastructure and expertise that were used in the terrorist campaigns remain intact. Specifically, manpower, weaponry, networks, knowledge, experience, secrecy, and efforts to build a reputation for toughness that made violent threats credible can cheaply and easily be put to use in serious and organized crime

Karen McElrath has shown that the heroin market has expanded greatly in Northern Ireland since the cease-fires in the mid-1990s. She offers a number of explanations for this, including a loosening of local and informal social control mechanisms that have allowed heroin to be more easily supplied in places where its use would have previously been closely policed by the paramilitaries.[3] Drug markets are often volatile and unstable. If no single group controls a monopoly and instead the market is composed of a larger number of individuals already predisposed to violence and competing intensely, then the drug trade will be particularly vulnerable to further outbreaks of violence.[4]

Strong and legitimate government that provides effective legal policing and protection is needed to prevent and combat organized crime. The dramatic shifts in the political landscape in Northern Ireland have laid the foundations for this, but it may be that the demand for certain goods and services such as cheap fuel are so strong that some forms of organized criminal activity are now entrenched.

To counterbalance this gloomy outlook, all aspects of serious and organized crime are disrupted by violence. In short, violence is bad for business. It can distract personnel from the business of making a profit, disrupt supply lines, make potential customers wary, and draw police attention to the activities of key individuals. It does not necessarily follow that an increase in organized crime will be accompanied by an increase in violence; it depends on the nature of the market.

The driving force behind this book was to investigate the puzzle as to why the certainty and severity of PPAs did not have a specific deterrent effect on a group of persistent offenders. In chapter 4, I sought to explain the hoods' seemingly irrational antisocial behavior by showing how their participation in various offenses and the mode of this participation can best be explained as a signaling game, played in order to attain and maintain prestige and status. The hoods do, of course, employ other signs and symbols of status such as clothes and tattoos, but these are easy to mimic, or, more precisely, the cost of having and displaying them are not high enough to prevent the non-hoods or lesser hoods from doing so.

Signaling theory has also been used to explain why PPAs have not deterred some hoods from reoffending, by showing how bearing the cost of a PPA has developed into an extremely discriminating signal of toughness among the hoods. It is therefore the experience of punishment and how one responds to it that truly differentiate those who are really tough from those whose criminality is on a lesser scale. If, as is hoped, PPAs cease, then the hoods will lose this way of distinguishing themselves from their peers. What will the implications of this be for their behavior?

Although PPAs may cease and the structure of the paramilitary groups may dissolve, the next generation of hoods who misuse substances and drop out of school will still be unable or very unlikely to attain status through education and employment. Roger Petersen has argued that in closed networks, status becomes incredibly important and that young males are generally more status conscious than any other demographic group.[5] Thus, the structural changes in the community will not dampen the desire for status among a relatively closed and tightly knit network of hoods.

Criminal prowess will continue to be associated with status and thus act as a semi-sorting signal, but the actual forms of criminality might change. Because of their youth and limiting resources, the crime and delinquency that most hoods participate in is likely to remain petty. However, if the costs of entry into the drug market are reduced and the market expands and becomes more financially lucrative, then participation in this market may become more accessible and attractive to younger offenders. Their ability to take part in buying and selling drugs will largely be determined by the way in which this market develops and the extent to which it becomes monopolized by individuals or groups.

A distinctive feature of the hoods in West Belfast has been their lack of gang structure. In my view, this has largely been determined by the IRA's strength and monopoly of violence. If the hoods had formed a structured, visible gang, they would have risked being seen as either opposing or competing with the IRA, which was larger, stronger, and more ruthless. Instead the hoods' survival has depended on their ad hoc relationships, loose coalitions, and short-term cooperation. If the IRA stands down, there is a greater probability that more recognizable gang-like structures may appear in West Belfast. These will have four main functions. First, the organizational structure will enable members to cooperate and participate more effectively in any emerging drug market or other criminal enterprises. Second, gangs provide young people with a sense of belonging and a peer group to identify with. Third, if gangs emerge, then young people will join in order to be protected from rival gangs. Fourth, the hierarchical structure and rules of behavior within a gang provide a forum within which status can be gained and maintained through fighting and involvement in criminal activities.

We have seen the importance that hoods place on participating publicly in delinquency and criminality. Their expressive displays of joyriding conveyed vital information about their traits to other hoods and to local people. However, these behaviors alone were not costly enough to discriminate between the tough and the truly tough. Nor did they provide the evidence that hoods needed about the trustworthiness of their peers. This information was partially conveyed through a period of imprisonment or more effectively by receiving a violent PPA. As PPAs cease, then existing or new behavior will develop into signals that act to discriminate between those truly in possession of status-enhancing characteristics. A signal can be any action that is costly to the person displaying the signal, but in order for it to be effective, those observing the signal must understand its meaning. However, there is a logical relationship between the signal and the message it conveys. Thus signs of toughness are most likely to involve the ability to endure physical pain and discomfort. If more structured gangs emerge, as predicted, then it is most likely that initiation rites such as "jump ins," where the new member is beaten (with his permission) by existing gang members, and formal positions within the gang hierarchy will develop into discriminating signals.

In Loyalist areas if the paramilitary structure remains, not much will change, as delinquent young people will continue to be absorbed into the existing armed groups involved in criminal activities.

NOTES

INTRODUCTION

1. "Joyriding the scourge returns," *Andersonstown News*, January 16, 1999.
2. "Fear stalks the streets," *Andersonstown News*, February 2, 1999.
3. Ibid.
4. "Call for action on joyriders in the wake of bus crash," *Andersonstown News*, September 25, 2000.
5. "The human cost of 'joyriding,'" *Irish News*, April 14, 2000.
6. One resident told the *Andersonstown News*, "The place is like Beirut here . . . from 8 pm on a Thursday night when there can be anything up to 100 kids drinking and causing trouble, burning out cars and terrorising local people. . . . They stand in massive gangs drinking and throwing stones." "Suffolk residents plead for proper policing to combat weekend anarchy." *Andersonstown News*, September 21, 2000.
7. Beale 1984: 629.
8. O'Connell 2006: 1.
9. Northern Ireland Office 1997: 1–2.
10. Ibid., 9. Also, results from the 2001 Census showed that 44 percent of the population of Northern Ireland described themselves as being brought up in a community background which was Catholic, while 53 percent of the population stated that they were brought up in a Protestant community background.
11. PSNI 2003, 2009.
12. Ibid.
13. IMC 2004: 25.
14. Hayes and McAllister 2001: 901.
15. For example, Oakley 1981: 35; Brannen 1988: 553; McCracken 1988: 9; Lee 1993.
16. "IRA survey raises householders' hackles,"*Andersonstown News*, November 17, 1998.
17. Humphreys 1970; Whyte 1981; Miles and Huberman 1994; Hammersley and Atkinson 1995.
18. Hammersley 1992; Hammersley and Atkinson 1995.
19. See also Brannen 1988.
20. Agar 1980: 456.
21. Wax and Cassell 1979.
22. Lee 1993: 103.

23. Varese 1996: 12.
24. Miles and Huberman 1994.
25. Hammersley and Atkinson 1995: 186.
26. Varese 1996: 13.
27. Silverman 1993; Yin, 1994.
28. Hammersley 1992: 69.
29. Ibid. 69.
30. Carney 2000.
31. Hammersley and Atkinson 1995: 230–231.
32. Cohen 1957: 13.
33. Emler and Reicher 1995: 46.
34. Matza 1964: 36–37.
35. Spence 1973; Frank 1988; Zahavi and Zahavi 1997.
36. Posner 2000: 5.

CHAPTER ONE
WEST BELFAST

1. The remaining 16.2 percent were from a "Protestant and Other Christian (including Christian related)" community background (Northern Ireland Statistics and Research Agency 2003).

2. In 2001, the population of the parliamentary constituency of West Belfast was 87,610, approximately 32 percent of the population of Belfast. Northern Ireland is a small country of 1,685,267 inhabitants; 43.8 percent were from a "Catholic" background and 53.1 percent were from a "Protestant and 'Other Christian' (including Christian related)" community background. Approximately 16 percent of the population live in Belfast, the capital city, and when the city suburbs are included, the number of inhabitants expands to almost one third of the total population of Northern Ireland (Northern Ireland Statistics and Research Agency 2003).

3. Northern Ireland is economically deprived compared with the rest of the United Kingdom. In 2002–03 its poverty rate was four percentage points above that in Britain in 1999 (Hillyard et al. 2003:31).

4. Northern Ireland Statistics and Research Agency 2005.

5. The more moderate nationalist party the Social Democratic and Labour Party (SDLP) came second in this election. Their candidate, Alex Attwood, won 14.57 percent of the vote.

6. The name of the city of Derry/Londonderry has caused a large amount of political contention. Nationalists favor the first term, Unionists favor the latter term.

7. Wilson 1996: 13–14.

8. Sutton 2010; Fay et al. 1999: 121.

9. Faye et al. 1999: 144.

10. Brewer et al. 1997: 171.

11. Leonard 1994: 109.

12. Leonard 2004: 933.

13. Posner 2000: 213.

14. Internment refers to the arrest and detention without trial of people suspected of being members of illegal paramilitary groups. In recent times, the policy was enacted between Monday, August 9, 1971 and Friday, December 5, 1975. During this period a total of 1,981 people were detained; 1,874 were Catholic/Republican, while 107 were Protestant/Loyalist (McGuffin 1973).

15. These are the colors of the flag of the Republic of Ireland, the symbol of a united Ireland.

16. On March 16, 1988, Michael Stone, a Loyalist paramilitary, attacked mourners at the funerals of the three IRA members shot dead by the Special Air Service (SAS), the special forces corps of the British army, in Gibraltar. Stone fired indiscriminately into the crowd gathered at Milltown Cemetery in West Belfast, killing three people.

17. During fieldwork, an article appeared in the *Andersonstown News*, a local West Belfast newspaper, warning residents not to respond to a questionnaire from the University of Luton containing questions relating to residents' religious beliefs and support for the Republican Movement. The article noted that these were "not the sort of queries you'd be inclined to post to a stranger in England" ("IRA survey raises householders' hackles,'" *Andersonstown News* [Belfast], November 17, 1998.

18. O'Connor 1993.

19. http://www.iol.ie/~wbelecon/; accessed August 5, 2005.

20. Ibid.

21. Noble et al. 2005.

22. These factors are paraphrased from McDonald 2001.

23. See Lewis 1989; Skogan 1994; Maguire 1997.

24. Northern Ireland Statistics and Research Agency 2005.

25. Brewer 1992.

26. Conway 1997: 109.

27. The "marching season" refers to the annual parades by the Protestant Orange Order that take place mostly in July and August. The Nationalists who live on the parade routes hotly contest many of these Loyalist parades, and the tension created often erupts into violence between the two sides. For a more detailed discussion, see Jarman and Bryan 1996.

28. Connolly 1998: 24.

29. "Joyriding protest takes to streets," *Irish News* [Belfast], September 18, 2000.

30. "Thugs named and shamed." *Andersonstown News* [Belfast], September 15, 2000.

31. See "Residents dig in to beat the weekend joyriders," *Irish News* [Belfast], July 28, 1997.

32. Hurley sticks are used to play the Irish sport of hurling and are like a cross between a baseball bat and a field hockey stick.

33. See "Joyride patrols welcomed. Spiked chains set to combat street racers," *Irish News* [Belfast], July 27, 1997.

34. "Joyriding scourge of the community," *An Phoblacht/Republican News* [Belfast], January 16, 1997.

35. Ibid.

36. A similar situation arose in Cape Town, South Africa, with the rise of People Against Gangsterism and Drugs (PAGAD) in predominantly Muslim neighborhoods. PAGAD began with well-intentioned local people trying to take a stand against crime in their closely knit communities. However, the organization soon became linked to a number of murders, bomb attacks, and armed robberies, and the South African government declared it a terrorist group ("PAGAD: Vigilantes or terrorists?" *BBC News*, Wednesday, September 13, 2000, available at http://news.bbc.co.uk/1/hi/world/africa/923701.stm. Accessed on November 20, 2006.

37. Human Rights Watch 1997: 118.

38. "Beating Denied by the IRA," *Irish News* [Belfast], March 29, 1996.

39. According to the Sunday Times Insight Team (1972: 49), the program of reform advocated by the Civil Rights Movement was as follows:

1. One-man-one-vote in local elections
2. The removal of gerrymandered boundaries
3. Laws against discrimination by local government, and the provision of machinery to deal with complaints
4. Allocation of public housing on a points system
5. Repeal of the Special Powers Act
6. Disbanding of the 'B' Specials

40. O'Connor 1993: 137.

41. O'Doherty 1998.

42. Fay et al. 1999a: 170.

43. Hayes and McAllister 2004: 57–58. The questions asked were as follows. "Now thinking about the reasons why some Loyalist groups have used violence during the Troubles, would you say that you have any sympathy with the reasons for violence, even if you don't condone the violence yourself? And, thinking about the reasons why some Republican groups have used violence during the Troubles, would you say that you have any sympathy with the reasons for violence, even if you don't condone the violence yourself?" (Northern Ireland and Republic of Ireland European Values Study 1999).

44. O'Connor 1993: 134.

45. Munck 1988: 86.

46. Burton 1978; Sluka, 1989. The murder of Robert McCartney outside Magennis's pub in Belfast in January 2005 is an example of public opinion turning away from the IRA. The IRA's offer to shoot those directly involved in the killing was rejected by the McCartney family, who demanded instead that there be cooperation with the police investigation (IRA statement published in *The Guardian*, March 8, 2005). The IRA subsequently expelled those linked to the murder from the organization (Neill 2005). The IMC have also suggested that because of the public outcry over Robert McCartney's murder, the IRA allowed some individuals who were previously exiled to return (IMC 2005b).

47. "IRA expels another tearaway," *Irish News*, August 30, 1999. The four teenagers expelled were from Dungannon.

48. Sluka 1989.

49. Silke and Taylor 2000: 268.

50. These courts grew out of the tradition of peasant "midnight courts," which were run by the early secret agrarian societies and those set up by the Irish Land League. Initially they were a pragmatic response to agrarian unrest that arose from disputes over land ownership and that often resulted in violence. Like all the earlier forms of alternative justice, the establishment of these courts was linked both to popular demands for self-help and to an increasingly extreme dissatisfaction with British law and the courts that enforced it (Bell 1996: 152). The courts began to multiply, peaking at 41 district and 900 parish courts, rendering more than 5,000 decisions. They were proving very successful in taking business away from the British court system (Townshend 1999: 92). In June 1920, the *Irish Times* declared that confidence in the sanctions of British law and order "vanished long ago, and [the] whole countryside now bring their rights and wrongs to the courts of Sinn Féin" (quoted in Connolly 1998: 19). Local IRA volunteers enforced the decisions of the courts and, here and there, they began to act as village constables.

51. Hillyard 1985: 250.

52. Munck 1988: 415–53.

53. Bell 1996: 158.

54. Conroy 1988: 35.

55. MacStiofáin 1975:124. The IRA had mounted campaigns in the 1930s, during World War II, and in the late 1950s, when the IRA, operating in the Republic of Ireland, launched attacks on targets on border with Northern Ireland. In 1962, the IRA called off the border campaign, admitting it had failed because it did not have the support of Catholics north or south. Some IRA men who had been active in the 1950s then drifted away from the organization as its leadership abandoned violence, agitated for social reform, and sold its weapons to Welsh

nationalists. The *Sunday Times* newspaper Insight Team quoted Cathal Goulding, former IRA Chief of Staff, saying,

> In August 1967 we called a meeting of local leadership throughout the country to assess the strength of the movement. We discovered that we had no movement." (Sunday Times Insight Team 1972: 26)

56. Hillyard 1985: 252; De Baróid, 2000: 26–27. In Belfast, a CCDC was formed for which each of the local committees selected a representative, and this central committee was responsible for developing and coordinating policy. It eventually consisted of 95 delegates representing 75,000 people in Belfast (Kelley 1982: 121).

57. Hillyard 1985: 252. Class divisions were soon to render the CCDC impotent and incidents such as an arson attack on three nationalist homes following the CCDC's persuasion or "coercion" of the residents on the lower Falls Road to take down their barricades in mid-September 1969 further discredited them in the eyes of West Belfast residents (de Baróid 1990: 33).

58. On August 9, 1971, in a series of raids across Northern Ireland by the British army and the RUC, 342 people were arrested and taken to makeshift camps. Internment was to continue until December 5, 1975, and during that time 1,981 people were detained: 1,874 were Catholic/Republican, while 107 were Protestant/Loyalist (McGuffin 1973). Many of those imprisoned were from West Belfast.

59. De Baróid 2000: 53.

60. Sunday Times Insight Team 1972: 238.

61. The following statement appeared in the *Ballymurphy News* (June 1974): "Republicans wish to appeal to drivers to observe speed limits on all roads and streets in the estate in an effort to reduce accident risk. There is no need for travelling up and down the Whiterock Road at 40-50 mph: such driving is reckless in the extreme and anyone apprehended by the Republican Movement for such action can expect to be dealt with severely. (The volume and number of this edition of the *Ballymurphy News* were not listed, but the document is archived in the Political Collection of the Linenhall Library, Belfast).

62. *Ballymurphy News*, December 1974. Belfast.

63. *Ballymurphy News* 4, no. 4, October 28, 1976. Belfast.

64. De Baróid 1990: 195–96.

65. The IRA issued the following statement after kneecapping a Belfast man:

> On the 6th July 1978, we carried out a punishment shooting of two men in the New Lodge Road area. On information then available, we were satisfied that they were guilty. However, new information had come to us which completely clears one of the men, Mr Edwards. Mr Edwards is a completely innocent man and we offer our sincerest apologies to him and his family. (*Republican News*, September 9, 1978; quoted in Kelley 1982: 290)

66. McKittrick 1999; "Bar killing follows bloody IRA pattern." *Irish News* [Belfast], February 28, 2005.

67. Kelley 1998.

68. Conroy 1988: 86.

69. Joe Austin, Sinn Féin Councillor quoted in Human Rights Watch, 1997: 126. The term 'boycott' originated in the system of informal justice that operated in the West of Ireland in the 19th century. The term was coined after Captain H. C. Boycott, the land agent for Lord Erne's estate in Lough Mask, Co County Mayo, endured the first organized campaign of ostracism (including the withdrawal of harvest labor) in the autumn of 1880 after a dispute over wages (Davitt 1904: 274).

70. The following report of the work of the People's Courts appeared in the June 1975 issue of the *Ballymurphy News* [Belfast] (The document is archived in the Political Collection of the Linenhall Library, Belfast.):

> On investigation and questioning of those involved and responsible for the attack, the Republican Movement decided, in keeping with the proposal in the last issue that People's Courts be established, to punish the offenders by making them brush streets in Springhill.
>
> Subsequently, attempted rapes took place in the same area and those previously punished were again involved. They have since been more severely dealt with. As a result of these incidents and also due to the amount of drinking which takes place in the cemetery, the Republican Movement has decided to resume patrols of the cemetery area at night. We bitterly regret that at a time when all our undivided energies and attention should be engaged in other directions, we have to divert personnel and time to prevent such antisocial behaviour by a very few people who are causing very grave problems.

71. Hillyard 1985.

72. Morrissey 1980.

73. De Baróid 2000: 172.

74. Ibid., 53.

75. Hillyard 1985: 257.

76. Martin McGuinness, "Belfast conference as Upper Springfield goes live," *An Phoblacht/Republican News*, March 18, 1999.

77. *An Phoblacht/Republican News*, August 26, 1982, quoted in Munck 1988: 47.

78. *An Phoblacht/Republican News*, February 2, 1984, quoted in Munck 1988: 48. An analysis of the crime rate at this time reveals an increase in crime in Northern Ireland as a whole by 12 percent between 1980 and 1983. This is compared with an increase of 36 percent in the Republic of Ireland over the same period (Heskin 1984: 191).

79. *An Phoblacht/Republican News*, February 16, 1984, quoted in Munck 1988: 49.

80. Sluka 1989.

81. In a letter to the *Andersonstown News*, the IRSP wrote, "The IRSP pledge to work with all those within local communities serious about tackling the local drug problems through community action and education. We see this as being a much more realistic and long-term strategy to combat drugs than a military threat that has more to do with short-term political expediency than an effective long-term strategy." See "Drug crime and dependency in the North and West," *Andersonstown News*, July 7, 2000.

82. Hillyard 1985: 249.

83. Ibid., 252.

84. Friedman 1962: 2.

85. In medieval Europe merchant guilds were established to resolve the contractual problems associated with long-distance trade. Government institutions did not exist to protect merchants and their property, so the guilds performed that function on their own (Greif et al. 1994; Greif 2006).

86. Dixit 2004: 128.

87. Varese 2006: 412.

88. Hill 2003: 15.

89. Dixit 2004: 25.

90. This figure is taken from the Magistrates Courts Annual Business Returns Report 2004 –2005.

91. Weitzer 1995: 178.

92. Coogan 1995: 126.

93. Weitzer 1995: 105.

94. *Andersonstown News*, October 24, 1998.

95. These trials throughout the 1980s were based entirely on the word of informers who were granted immunity from prosecution for the crimes they had committed, including involvement in killings, in return for their evidence. It was subsequently revealed that those providing evidence were also offered substantial sums of money in return for their testimony.

96. Dunn et al. 2000.

97. Howe 1990.

98. Leonard 1994: 186.

99. Dixit 2004.

100. In North Belfast in 2004–2005 the clearance rate was 20.5 percent, and in 2005–2006 it was 23.1 percent. In West Belfast in 2004–2005, the clearance rate was 22.8 percent, and in 2005–2006 it was 22.1 percent (Police Service for Northern Ireland 2006a).

101. Kennedy 1995.

102. Gambetta 1993: 251.

103. Tvetkova 2008.

104. Knox 2002: 174.

105. McGuigan was released in 1998 under the terms of the Good Friday Agreement. He served five years of his twelve-year sentence (Moriarty 1998).

106. Human Rights Watch 1997: 110.

107. Monaghan 2004: 443.

108. Silke 1999: 22.

109. See Gambetta 2009.

110. Silke and Taylor 2000.

111. Silke 1999.

112. Kennedy 1995: 78.

113. Quoted in Human Rights Watch 1997: 108.

114. Burton 1978: 110.

CHAPTER TWO
THE HOODS

1. Northern Ireland Statistics and Research Agency (2003).

2. Poland 2000.

3. The Self-Reported Delinquency study carried out in Belfast showed that delinquency was widespread among young people, but much of it was of a minor nature and of low intensity. However, there was a minority who reported offending more than 50 times per year, especially in the drug and violence categories (McQuoid 1994).

4. Little et al. 2004: 226.

5. Wolfgang et al. 1972; Hagell and Newburn 1994; Graham and Bowling 1995; Farrington 1997; Rutter et al. 1998.

6. Little et al. 2004.

7. Rea 1994: 45.

8. A caller claiming to represent the IRA and using a recognized codeword told a local newspaper that the group had nothing to do with the assault on Mary.

9. Hobbs 1997: 812; Patrick 1973: 102–13.

10. Campbell 1990: 167.

11. Lofland 1969: 91, quoted in Wright and Decker 1994: 205.

12. Nicholas et al. 1993: 90.

13. "Loyalists warn off 'Catholic' thieves,'" *Irish News* [Belfast], June 20, 1998.

14. Ibid.

15. One of the most infamous cases occurred in September 1990. Martin Peake (age 17) and Karen Reilly (age 18) were shot at and killed when they raced their Vauxhall Astra through a British army security checkpoint. Lee Clegg, the paratrooper initially convicted of murdering Miss Reilly, and wounding Mr. Peake, had his conviction overturned by the Court of Appeal in February 2000 (Watt 2000).

16. "Taxis face weekend of joyrider terrorism," *Irish News* [Belfast], April 17, 1999.

17. See also D. Gambetta and H. Hamill, *Streetwise: How taxi drivers establish customer's trustworthiness* (New York: Russell Sage Foundation, 2005).

18. See "Youth held after 100 mph 'joyriding,'" *Irish News* [Belfast] July 17, 1999.

19. Mr. Moore and his family were intimidated for a year by hoods who believed that he was a member of a vigilante group established to combat joyriding in that area. The *Irish News* reported that a gang of four rammed the family's car and smashed the windows with a crowbar. During the attack they shouted abuse at the family. Mr. Moore denied the allegations, but his protests did not stop the joyriders. Such incidents are not isolated, and others have suffered similarly. See "Joyriders terrorise family—Nightmare victim is not a vigilante," *Irish News* [Belfast], February 10, 1997.

20. The 1988 British Crime Survey found that those most at risk of being a victim of an assault are men who are single and under 30 years old, drink heavily several evenings a week, and assault others (Zedner 1997: 581–82).

21. Research into the effects of drugs and alcohol confirms that while they are mood altering, there is no determination as to what that mood will be (see South 2002).

22. During the fieldwork period this included the Driving Away Team and the Team for Auto Crime.

23. Data received from the Statistics and Research Unit, Northern Ireland Office, November, 24, 2004.

24. *Belfast Telegraph*, November 10, 1998.

25. Republican Movement Information Leaflet: February 1989. Source: Linenhall Library, Belfast, quoted by Knox 2002: 173.

26. Human Rights Watch 1997: 39.

27. Quoted in ibid., 126.

28. Conway 1994.

29. "Attack victim 'defied' IRA exile," *Irish News* [Belfast], May 3, 2000.

30. Thompson and Mulholland 1995: 56.

31. See "Attack victim 'defied' IRA exile." A few weeks after being attacked, Paul McDonald was killed in a car accident. See "IRA punishment victim killed in horror smash," *Irish News* [Belfast], June 19, 2000.

32. Thompson and Mulholland 1995: 55.

33. Cumann na mBan is the women's wing of the IRA and is believed to play a mainly supporting role in IRA activities (University of Ulster, Conflict Archive on the Internet (CAIN), The Northern Ireland Conflict: 1968 to the Present, available at http://cain.ulst.ac.uk/othelem/organ/corgan.htm. Accessed March 14, 2010.

34. Bell 1996: 156.

35. Barr and Mullan 1989: 875.

36. Jeff Maxwell, Base 2, quoted in Human Rights Watch 1997: 114.

37. Kelley 1982: 291.

38. This is a reference to an Italian Catholic priest who had stigmata on his hands (McKittrick 2005).

39. "Official IRA behind Turf Lodge shooting," *Andersonstown News* [Belfast], April 15, 2000.

40. For a particularly graphic account of a tarring and feathering incident, see the description in Robert McLiam Wilson's 1989 novel *Ripley Bogle* (London: Minerva, 1997), 111–14.

41. Conroy 1988: 87.

42. Burton 1978: 109.

43. Conroy 1988: 87.

44. "Attack on girl breaches cease-fire," *The Times*, October 27, 1995.

45. Derry Women's Aid refused to distinguish between violence against women, whether it was at the hands of Republican paramilitaries, the RUC or army, or husbands, regardless of the alleged offense. They provided practical aid to victims of paramilitary punishments and publicly demanded that such attacks should cease. In Derry, there was a noticeable decrease in punishment attacks on women, and Women's Aid believes that while there is no guarantee that the confrontation had any lasting effect on the ideas of local paramilitaries, it ensured that attacks on women could give rise to considerable public criticism and therefore should not be undertaken lightly (Harkin and Kilmurray 1985: 42)

46. Harkin and Kilmurray 1985: 42. In 1987 the IRA issued an additional Code of Conduct which states the following:

> Republicanism stands for equality and an end to sexism. Male volunteers who mistreat or exploit their partners are flying in the face of this principle. Volunteers must practice domestically what the movement preaches publicly." (quoted in Dillon 1996: 380).

47. Canning 2005.

48. Thompson and Mulholland 1995: 57.

49. Ibid. 53.

50. Murphy 2001.

51. Of the 22 percent who admitted to attempting suicide at least once, 19 percent had attempted to hang themselves, 50 percent had slit their wrists, and 31 percent had taken a drug overdose. In 1995 Malachy Clarke committed suicide by hanging himself in his home. In a newspaper interview, his father, Thomas Clarke, stated,

> The fact is that my son was viciously beaten by known IRA paramilitaries and continually intimidated right up to his death. . . . There was continual intimidation by those so-called heroes or vigilantes who administer justice in their own form.

Thomas Clarke blamed the IRA's actions for Malachy's death and quoted his son's suicide note as proof: "Do not feel it is your fault as it is not. It is the dirty stinking piggy rats out on the street" (quoted in Human Rights Watch 1997: 129). In a similar case in 1997, 21-year-old Gerard Marley hanged himself from railings near the Westlink motorway that skirts the edge of West Belfast. In the newspaper reports that followed Gerard's death, his father disclosed that his son had been a joyrider and had sustained two punishment beatings from the IRA that destroyed both his legs. He also had to put up with jeers and taunts from Republicans because he walked with a limp as a result of the assaults. According to Gerard's father, "the mental scars refused to heal—and constant taunts pushed him to end his life."

52. Thompson and Mulholland 1995: 60.

CHAPTER THREE
SEARCH FOR STATUS

1. Elster 1999: 203.
2. Ibid.
3. Petersen 2001: 20–21.
4. Coogan 1993.
5. McWilliams, 1995: 15–20.
6. Silke 1999: 15.
7. Williams was just 19 years old when he was hanged in Crumlin Road jail, Belfast, for his involvement in the murder of an RUC constable in 1942. Supporters had campaigned for over fifty years to have his remains taken from inside the walls of Crumlin Road jail and reburied in West Belfast ("Body's return is appropriate," *Irish News*, August 28, 1999).
8. Picard 1991.
9. The Blanket Protest refers to the first stage of the protest against criminal status by both Republican and Loyalist inmates in the Maze Prison between 1976 and 1981. Prisoners hoped to achieve political status by refusing to wear prison clothing and chose instead to covering themselves with blankets. In 1980 Republicans escalated this protest into the Hunger Strikes. The aim of the Hunger Strikes was to gain the reintroduction of "political" status for Republican prisoners. Special-category, or "political," status involved the following: the right of prisoners to wear their civilian clothes at all times; the right to free association within a block of cells; the right not to do prison work; the right to educational and recreational facilities; and the restoration of lost remission of sentence. In total, ten men starved themselves to death during the protest (see Beresford 1987; Campbell et al. 1994).
10. Bobby Sands, the then-leader of the IRA in the Maze Prison, became the most famous IRA Hunger Striker. On April 11, 1981, during the Hunger Strike, Sands was elected MP during a by-election for the Fermanagh/South Tyrone seat.

Bobby Sands died in the Maze Prison on May 5, 1981 (see Beresford 1987; Campbell et al. 1994).

11. The mural included portraits of Irish Republican Hunger Strikers Frank Stagg (died 1976); Michael Gaughan (died 1974); Nora Connolly, civil rights activist and daughter of 1916 Easter Rising leader, James Connolly (died 1981); Mairéad Farrell, an Irish Republican who went on hunger strike in Armagh women's prison and was shot dead by the SAS in Gibraltar, 1988, along with Sean Savage and Daniel McCann. Their portraits appeared alongside Dr. Martin Luther King, Jr., the American civil rights activist; Leonard Peltier, a Native American civil rights activist; Nelson Mandela; and Mohandas "Mahatma" Ghandi. For more information, see http://cain.ulst.ac.uk/mccormick/album27.htm (accessed March 14, 2010) and Holland and McDonald (2001).

12. A further public display of loyalty to the Republican Movement and, by association, the possession of all the valued and honorable traits associated with being a Republican, is the ability to speak Irish. Republican prisoners in the Maze Prison learned Irish for a number of reasons: it was one way to relieve the boredom of prison life; it promoted a greater sense of nationality and solidarity; and the prison guards were unable to understand it. Irish became the language of resistance within the Maze Prison, and knowledge of the Irish language in West Belfast implies strong allegiance to Republicanism.

13. See http://cain.ulst.ac.uk/othelem/organ/iorgan.htm.

14. Bell 1990: 6.

15. Also translated as "Republican Scouts."

16. McCullough et al. 1990: 3.

17. Schneider 1999: 93–94.

18. O'Connor 1993: 130–31.

19. Cohen 1957: 59.

20. Patrick 1973; Parker 1974; Gill 1977; Bourgois 2003.

21. Hobbs 1997: 808.

22. Mays 1954; Parker 1974.

23. Howe 1990: 47–68.

24. Hobbs 1997: 809.

25. Ibid., 807.

26. Ibid.

27. Rock 1997: 238.

28. Ibid., 237.

29. Farrington 1997.

30. "Things were different when I was young," *Andersonstown News* [Belfast], November 1, 2000.

31. "Killed joyrider's mum meets crash orphan," *Irish News* [Belfast], January 21, 2000.

32. O'Doherty 1998: 151.

33. "Widow defies threats by drug campaigners," *Irish News* [Belfast], November 5, 1998.

34. Coleman and Hendry 1990.

35. Emler and Reicher 1995: 57.

36. The three primary reasons why these young people were excluded from school were violence against other pupils or teachers (38%), truancy (28%), and vandalism (15%).

37. Wright and Decker 1994: 40.

38. See "Gang attacks cars and school minibus during drug inspired rampage. Thugs bring terror to estate residents," *Irish News* [Belfast], March 1, 1996.

39. Spergel 1992.

40. Cohen 1990: 8.

41. Maxson and Klein 1990.

42. Jankowski 1991: 28–29.

43. Spergel 1992.

44. Venkatesh 2000: 134.

45. Venkatesh and Levitt 2000: 456.

46. Klein 1995: 58–59.

47. Jankowski 1991: 29.

48. Cohen and Short 1958.

49. Cloward and Ohlin 1960.

50. Gold 1970: 92.

51. Ibid., 94.

52. Following attacks that saw one member of the IPLO killed and eight others injured by the IRA, the IPLO announced that it was disbanding in 1992.

53. Jankowski 1991: 44.

54. Wright and Decker 1994: 76

Chapter Four
Signaling Games

1. Wright and Decker 1994: 42.

2. Bacharach and Gambetta 2001.

3. Gambetta and Hamill 2005.

4. Spence 1973.

5. Zahavi 1975.

6. Akerlof 1970; Spence 1973: 2002.

7. Zahavi and Zahavi 1997.

8. Bliege Bird and Smith 2005.

9. Gambetta 2009; Gambetta and Hamill 2005.

10. Levi 1997: 881.

11. Steve Bruce (1992: 186) also makes this point when explaining the brutality of a Loyalist terror gang called the Shankill Butchers.

12. Veblen ([1899] 1970: 167) identified this trait when he noted that

there is in all countries a similar, though less formal, social obligation incumbent on the rowdy to assert his manhood in unprovoked combat with his fellows. . . . The boy usually knows to a nicety, from day to day, how he and his associates grade in respect of relative fighting capacity; and in the community of boys there is ordinarily no secure basis of reputability for any one who, by exception, will not or can not fight on invitation.

13. As Veblen ([1899] 1970: 170) put it, such fights are "to be classed under the head of exploit. They are partly simple and unreflected expressions of an attitude of emulative ferocity, partly activities deliberately entered upon with a view to gaining repute for prowess."

14. Hughes and Short 2005: 61.

15. Frank 1985: 104.

16. Zahavi and Zahavi 1997: 8.

17. Herrnstein 1995.

18. Fagan 1990.

19. Katz 1988: 52.

20. "Joyrider Video in Schools," *Andersonstown News* [Belfast], March 15, 2000.

21. Ibid.

22. Maguire 1982; Shover and Honaker 1992; Wright and Decker 1994.

23. Farrington 1997: 381.

24. Personal communication with Diego Gambetta.

25. Wright and Decker 1994: 42.

26. Felman and Santora 1981.

27. Department of Health, Social Services and Public Safety, 2005. See also "Teenage Mums Shock Revealed," *Belfast Telegraph*, September 9, 2000.

28. Von Hirsch et al. 1999: 6.

29. Ibid.

30. Thompson and Mulholland 1995: 56.

31. Hamill 1999: vii.

32. "Shooting Tactics Resume in City," *Irish News* [Belfast], June 21, 2000.

33. Thompson and Mulholland 1995: 57.

34. Ibid.

35. "Three Forced to Queue in Shooting Horror," *Belfast Telegraph*, October 29, 1996.

36. See Kennedy 2001.

37. McAleer 1994: 149.

CHAPTER FIVE
LOYALISTS

1. 4.1 percent of the population in Northern Ireland are registered unemployed, and of those, 40.4 percent are long-term unemployed. In Falls/Clonard, 8.6 percent of the population are registered unemployed, and of those, 46.7 percent are long-term unemployed. In the Greater Shankill 7.7 percent of the population are registered unemployed, and of those, 51.4 percent are long-term unemployed (Northern Ireland Statistics and Research Agency 2005).

2. Wilson 1996: 63.

3. http://cain.ulst.ac.uk/othelem/organ/uorgan.htm#uda. Accessed January 15, 2007.

4. Sutton 2002.

5. Between 2000 and 2003, there were almost 500 pipe bomb attacks against Catholics, most of which were carried out by the UDA. This is an average of an attack every two days in this period (O'Neill 2003).

6. http://cain.ulst.ac.uk/othelem/organ/uorgan.htm#uda. Accessed January 15, 2007.

7. The RHC is a small Loyalist paramilitary group. It was formed in 1972 and was declared illegal in 1973.

8. Sutton 2010.

9. Bruce 1992: 127.

10. Monaghan 2004: 442; McCaffrey 2004.

11. Jarman 2004: 421.

12. McCaffrey 2004. Johnny Adair rose through the ranks of the UDA to become Brigadier 2nd Battalion, C Company and effectively control the UDA in West Belfast. Convicted for the offense of directing terrorism, he is thought to have been responsible for the murders of twenty Catholics (Bruce 2004: 512–17).

13. Bruce 2004: 505.

14. Fay et al. 1999: 153. The area contains eight of the official Belfast Peace Lines, and the area is a patchwork quilt of small communities bounded by interface areas (North Belfast Advice Consortium 1999).

15. Hayes and McAllister 2001: 909.

16. The Ulster Defence Regiment was established in 1970 and was a locally recruited branch of the British army. It was merged with the Royal Irish Rangers in 1992. It was an almost exclusively Protestant organization, and at the time of its merger its membership was only 3 percent Catholic.

17. Those responsible for the remaining thirty (2 percent) deaths are classified as unknown (Sutton 2002).

18. Hayes and McAllister 2001: 917.

19. Taylor 2000: 77.

20. Nelson 1984.

21. At the time of writing, these programs are in North Belfast, East Belfast, and the Kilcooley Estate in Bangor.

22. At the time of this writing, these programs are in South Armagh and Newry.

23. Northern Ireland Affairs Committee 2006.

24. Between July 7 and 9, 1999, the police and army fired over 1660 plastic bullets during Loyalist parades (Devenport 2000).

25. Brewer 1992.

26. Nelson 1984: 88.

27. PSNI 2006a.

28. Bruce 1992: 275.

29. Silke and Taylor 2000: 263.

30. PSNI 2006a.

31. The share of the vote in the 2005 Westminster Elections was as follows: DUP 33.71 percent; Sinn Féin 24.32 percent; UUP 17.74 percent; and SDLP 17.51 percent.

32. This seat was held by David Ervine in Belfast East.

33. McKittrick 2007.

34. Winston 1997: 124–25.

35. In 2002, the police had to abandon plans for a weekly community policing clinic on the Protestant Rathcoole estate. The building that was to be used for the clinic was daubed with graffiti about "touts," and a pipe bomb was placed under the car of a local councillor who supported the initiative (Gordon 2002).

36. Nelson 1984: 88.

37. Murray 2003.

38. See Stevens Report (2003). Bruce (2004) argues that the collusion between Loyalists and the security forces has given credence to their attempts to legitimize their violence by demonstrating that they have men within their ranks who have served their country in a more "official" capacity.

39. See the Stevens Report on British Intelligence's Force Research Unit and RUC Special Branch and, more recently, the O'Loan report. Lister and Jordan (2003: 126) allege that Johnny Adair used to openly drive around nationalist districts to spy on targets. If stopped at the many security vehicle checkpoints, he would receive from soldiers and police the names, addresses, and information on recent sightings of IRA men and their associates.

40. IMC 2005a: 21–22.

41. Bruce 1992: 276.

42. Between 1971 and 1972 the capture of Catholics and their subsequent torture and killing in Loyalist clubs became known as "rompering" after a local children's television program called "Romper Room." The terms first became used in public during the trial of seven UDA men for the murder of 21-year-old East Belfast Catholic James Patrick McCartan (McDonald and Cusack 2004: 55).

43. Silke 2000: 113.
44. McDonald 1996.
45. McCaffrey 2003b.
46. Silke and Taylor 2000: 256.
47. Select Committee on Northern Ireland Affairs 2001.
48. McCaffrey 2003a.
49. Murray 2002.
50. IMC 2007b.
51. IMC 2007a.
52. Cowan 2002; Lister and Jordan 2003: 311.
53. *Belfast News Letter*, August 9, 2002.
54. Northern Ireland Office 1997.
55. The youth wing of the UDA is called the Ulster Young Militants (UYM), and the youth wing of UVF is called the Young Citizen Volunteers (YCV).

CONCLUSION

1. IMC 2007b.
2. Gambetta 1993: 252.
3. McElrath 2004.
4. Ousey and Lee 2004. Venkatesh and Levitt (2000: 462) note that in their study of a Chicago drug gang, the annual death rate among gang members was 4.2 percent, more than 100 times the national average for African American males in this age group. An analysis of a subset of the gang revealed that each member had a 25 percent chance of dying if he remained a member of the gang over a four-year period and if all members stayed the same during that time. On average, a drug seller could expect 0.59 wounds (virtually all from bullets) and 1.43 arrests per year.
5. Petersen 2001: 20–21; 48.

GLOSSARY OF TERMS

Central Citizens' Defence Committee (CCDC) — established in 1969 in West Belfast, the CCDC amalgamated a number of community and defense groups.

Combined Loyalist Military Command (CLMC) — established in 1991, this umbrella organization attempted to coordinate the activities of all the Loyalist paramilitary groups particularly with regard to announcing a cease-fire in 1994.

Continuity Irish Republican Army (CIRA) — a Republican paramilitary group made up of former members of other Republican groups, especially the IRA. They came to prominence in 1996 and have been opposed to the peace process and IRA cease-fire.

Cumann na mBan — the female wing of the Irish Republican Army (IRA).

Democratic Unionist Party (DUP) — the largest, and more conservative, of the two main Unionist political parties in Northern Ireland. The DUP's leader is the Reverend Ian Paisley.

Direct Action Against Drugs (DAAD) — a vigilante organization that appeared in 1994 and claimed responsibility for the deaths of a number of alleged drug dealers.

Independent Monitoring Commission (IMC) — established in 2003 by the British and Irish governments, the IMC reports on the commitments made in the Good Friday Agreement with regard to paramilitary activity, security normalization, and participation in the political institutions.

Irish National Liberation Army (INLA) — a Republican paramilitary group that was established in 1975.

Irish People's Liberation Organisation (IPLO) — a group that began as a breakaway faction from the Irish National Liberation Army (INLA). It disbanded in 1992.

Irish Republican Army (IRA) — the main Republican paramilitary group in Northern Ireland. Also known as the Provisional Irish Republican Army (PIRA).

Loyalist Volunteer Force (LVF) — formed in 1996 from disaffected members of the mid-Ulster brigade of the Ulster Volunteer Force (UVF) and disbanded in 2005.

Official Irish Republican Army (OIRA) — the name adopted by those in the IRA who did not join the Provisional Irish Republican Army (PIRA) following a split in 1970.

Police Service of Northern Ireland (PSNI) — formerly the Royal Ulster Constabulary (RUC).

Paramilitary Punishment Attack (PPA) — name given to a nonmilitary violent attack by Republican and Loyalist paramilitary groups on a member of their own community.

Progressive Unionist Party (PUP) — a small Loyalist political party that has links with the Ulster Volunteer Force (UVF).

"real" Irish Republican Army (rIRA) — established in 1997, this Republican paramilitary group was formed by dissident members of the Irish Republican Army (IRA) who were opposed to the "peace process" and the political leadership of Sinn Féin.

Red Hand Commando (RHC) — established in 1972, this small Loyalist paramilitary group is closely associated with the Ulster Volunteer Force (UVF).

Red Hand Defenders (RHD) — a Loyalist paramilitary grouping that first appeared in 1998. It is believed that members are drawn from the Loyalist Volunteer Force (LVF), and also elements of the Ulster Defence Association (UDA).

Royal Ulster Constabulary (RUC) — the name of the Northern Ireland police service from June 1922 to November 2001. Its name was then changed to the Police Service of Northern Ireland (PSNI).

Ulster Defence Association (UDA) — formed in 1971, the UDA is the largest Loyalist paramilitary group in Northern Ireland.

Ulster Defence Regiment (UDR) — operational between 1970 and 1992, when it was merged with the Royal Irish Rangers, the UDR was a locally recruited regiment of the British army. Its membership was almost exclusively Protestant—only 3 percent of its members were Catholic.

Ulster Democratic Party (UDP) — formed in 1981, the UDP sought to be the political voice of, and to offer political advise to, the UDA. It performed poorly in elections and was dissolved in 2001.

Ulster Freedom Fighters (UFF) — cover name used by the Ulster Defence Association (UDA).

Ulster Unionist Party (UUP) — second largest of the two main Unionist political parties in Northern Ireland.

Ulster Volunteer Force (UVF) — established in 1966, the UVF is the second-largest Loyalist paramilitary group in Northern Ireland.

BIBLIOGRAPHY

Newspaper Reports

An Phoblacht. January 16, 1997. "Joyriding scourge of the community," *An Phoblacht/Republican News*. Belfast.

Andersonstown News. November 17, 1998. "IRA survey raises householders' hackles." in *Andersonstown News*. Belfast.

———. January 16, 1999. "Joyriding: The scourge returns." *Andersonstown News*. Belfast.

———. February 2, 1999. "Fear stalks the streets." *Andersonstown News*. Belfast.

———. March 15, 2000. "Joyrider Video in Schools." *Andersonstown News*. Belfast.

———. April 15, 2000. "Official IRA behind Turf Lodge shooting." *Andersonstown News*. Belfast.

———. July 7, 2000. "Drug crime and dependency in the North and West." *Andersonstown News*. Belfast.

———. July 27, 2000. "Ruthless trap was aimed at snaring jobless man." *Andersonstown News*. Belfast.

———. September 15, 2000. "Thugs named and shamed." *Andersonstown News*. Belfast.

———. September 21, 2000. "Suffolk residents plead for proper policing to combat weekend anarchy." *Andersonstown News*. Belfast.

———. September 25, 2000. "Call for action on joyriders in the wake of bus crash." *Andersonstown News*. Belfast.

Ballymurphy News. December 1974. *Ballymurphy News*. Belfast.

———. June 1975. *Ballymurphy News*. Belfast.

———. October 28, 1976. *Ballymurphy News* 4. Belfast.

Belfast News Letter. December 22, 2000. "Teenagers the prize in terror recruits drive." *Belfast News Letter (Northern Ireland)*. Belfast.

———. August 9, 2002. "'Adair may have been in dark on attack'; Loyalist chief's son is victim of punishment shooting." *Belfast News Letter (Northern Ireland)*. Belfast.

Belfast Telegraph. October 29, 1996. "Three forced to queue in shooting horror." *Belfast Telegraph*. Belfast.

———. September 9, 2000. "Teenage Mums' Shock Revealed." *Belfast Telegraph*. Belfast.

Irish News. March 29, 1996. "Beating Denied by the IRA," *Irish News*. Belfast.

———. April 2, 1996. "Inhumanity of gang beatings." *Irish News*. Belfast.

———. February 10, 1997. "Joyriders terrorise family—Nightmare victim is not a vigilante." *Irish News*. Belfast.

Irish News. July 27, 1997. "Joyride patrols welcomed. Spiked chains set to combat street racers." *Irish News*. Belfast.

———. July 28, 1997. "Residents dig in to beat the weekend joyriders." *Irish News*. Belfast.

———. June 20, 1998. "Loyalists warn off 'Catholic Thieves.'" *Irish News*. Belfast.

———. April 17, 1999. "Taxis face weekend of joyrider terrorism." *Irish News*. Belfast.

———. July 17, 1999. "Youth held after 100 mph 'joyriding.'" *Irish News*. Belfast.

———. August 30, 1999. "IRA expels another tearaway," *Irish News*. Belfast.

———. April 14, 2000. "The human cost of 'joyriding,'" *Irish News*. Belfast.

———. May 3, 2000. "Attack victim 'defied' IRA exile." in *Irish News*. Belfast.

———. June 19, 2000. "IRA punishment victim killed in horror smash." *Irish News*. Belfast.

———. September 18, 2000. "Joyriding protest takes to streets." *Irish News*. Belfast.

———. February 28, 2005. "Bar killing follows bloody IRA pattern." Irish News. Belfast.

The Times [London]. October 27, 1995. "Attack on girl breaches cease-fire." *The Times*. London.

Books and Articles

Adams, G. 1996. *Before the Dawn: An Autobiography*. London: Heinemann in association with Brandon Books.

Adams, J. 1986. *The Financing of Terror*. London: Hodder and Stoughton.

Agar, M. 1980. *Professional Stranger*. New York: Academic Press.

Amelin, K., M. Willis, C. Blair, and D. Donnelly. 2000. "Attitudes to Crime, Crime Reduction and Community Safety in Northern Ireland. Review of the Criminal Justice System in Northern Ireland Report 1." Belfast, Northern Ireland: Northern Ireland Office, Statistics and Research Branch.

Anderson, E. 1992. *Streetwise: Race, Class, and Change in an Urban Community*. Chicago: University of Chicago Press.

Bacharach, M., and D. Gambetta. 2001. "Trust in Signs." In *Trust in Society*, edited by K. Cook. New York: Russell Sage Foundation.

Bairner, A. 1996. "Paramilitarism." In *Northern Ireland Politics*, edited by A Aughey and D. Morrow. London: Longman.

Barr, R. J., and R.A.B Mullan. 1989. "Kneecapping: A misnomer." *Journal of Bone and Joint Surgery* 71-B: 875–80.

Beale, P., ed. 1984. *A Dictionary of Slang and Unconventional Language*. London: Routledge and Kegan Paul.

Becker, G. 1968. "Crime and Punishment: An Economic Approach." *Journal of Political Economy* 76 (March/April): 169–217.

Bell, C. 1996. "Alternative Justice in Ireland." In *One Hundred and Fifty Years of Irish Law*, edited by N. Dawson, G. Greer, and P. Ingram. Dublin: Round Hall Sweet & Maxwell.

Bell, D. 1990. *Acts of Union: Youth Culture and Sectarianism in Northern Ireland*. Basingstoke, England: Macmillan.

Bennett, T., and R. Wright. 1984. *Burglars on Burglary: Prevention and the Offender*. Aldershot, England: Gower.

Beresford, D. 1987. Ten Men Dead: The Story of the 1981 Irish Hunger Strike. London: Grafton.

Bliege Bird, R. and E. A. Smith. 2005. "Signaling Theory, Strategic Interaction and Symbolic Capital." *Current Anthropology* 46, no. 2 (April): 221–48.

Bourgois, P. I. 2003. In Search of Respect: Selling Crack in El Barrio. 2nd ed. New York: Cambridge University Press.

Braithwaite, J. 1989. *Crime, Shame and Reintegration*. Cambridge: Cambridge University Press.

Brannen, J. 1988. "The Study of Sensitive Subjects." *Sociological Review* 36, no. 3 (August): 552–63.

Brewer, J. D. 1992. "The Public and the Police." In *Social Attitudes in Northern Ireland: The Second Report*, edited by P. Stringer and G. Robinson. Belfast, Northern Ireland: Blackstaff.

Brewer, J. D., B. Lockhart, and P. Rodgers. 1997. *Crime in Ireland 1945–95: 'Here Be Dragons.'* Oxford: Clarendon.

Brewer, J. D., with K. Magee. 1991. *Inside the RUC. Routine Policing in a Divided Society*. Oxford: Clarendon Press.

Briggs, J. 1991. "A Profile of the Juvenile Joyrider and a Consideration of Motor Vehicle Projects as a Diversionary Strategy." M.A. thesis. University of Durham, Department of Sociology and Social Policy.

Bruce, S. 1992. *The Red Hand: Protestant Paramilitaries in Northern Ireland*. Oxford: Oxford University Press.

———. 2001. "Terrorists and Politics: The Case of Northern Ireland's Loyalist Paramilitaries." *Terrorism and Political Violence* 13, no. 2: 27–48.

———. 2004. "Turf War and Peace: Loyalist Paramilitaries since 1994." *Terrorism and Political Violence* 16, no. 3: 501–21.

Burton, F. 1978. *The Politics of Legitimacy: Struggles in a Belfast Community*. London: Routledge and Kegan Paul.

Campbell, A. 1990. "Female Participation in Gangs." Pp. 163–82 in *Gangs in America*, edited by C. R. Huff. London: Sage Publications.

Campbell, B., L. McKeown, and F. O'Hagan, eds. 1994. Nor Meekly Serve My Time: The H-block Struggle 1976–1981. Belfast, Northern Ireland: Beyond the Pale.

Canning, M. 2005. "Sickening Violence against Children—Shaming Attacks 'Best of Bad Lot.'" *Irish News* [Belfast]. August 12.

Carney, S. 2000. "Professional Development from School-Based Initial Teacher Training: Possibilities and Constraints for Schools." D.Phil. diss., Department of Educational Studies, University of Oxford.

Clarke, L., and V. Kearney. 1999. "Hard-hitting Clinton tells Adams 'IRA must end war'" *Sunday Times* [London]. March 21.

Cloward, R. A., and L. E. Ohlin. 1960. *Delinquency and Opportunity: A Theory of Delinquent Gangs*. New York: Free Press.

Cohen, A. 1957. *Delinquent Boys*. Glencoe, Ill.: Free Press.

———. 1990. "Introduction." In *Gangs in America*, edited by C. R Huff. London: Sage Publications.

Cohen, A. K., and F. Short, Jr. 1958. "Research in Delinquent Subcultures." *Journal of Social Issues* 14, no. 3 (September): 20–37.

Coleman, J. C., and L. Hendry. 1990. *The Nature of Adolescence*. London: Routledge.

Coleman, J. S. 1994. "The Realization of Effective Norms." Pp. 171–89 in *Four Sociological Traditions. Selected Readings*, edited by R. Collins. Oxford: Oxford University Press.

Connolly, S. J., ed. 1998. *The Oxford Companion to Irish History*. Oxford: Oxford University Press.

Conroy, J. 1988. *War as a Way of Life. A Belfast Diary*. London: Heinemann.

Conway, P. 1994. "Development of a Service-Based Response to Those under Threat from Paramilitaries in Northern Ireland." M.A. thesis. Faculty of Economics and Social Sciences, Queens University Belfast.

———1997. "Critical Reflections: A Response to Paramilitary Policing in Northern Ireland." *Critical Criminology* 8: 109–21.

Coogan, T. P. 1993. *The I.R.A.* Rev. and exp. ed. London: HarperCollins.

———. 1995. *The Troubles: Ireland's Ordeal 1966–1995 and the Search for Peace*. London: Hutchinson.

Cowan, R. 2002. "Adair's son takes his punishment: A shooting sanctioned by his father. Youth accused of 'raising his fists' returns home to nurse leg wounds." *The Guardian* [London]. August 9.

Darby, J. 1974. "Intimidation in Housing: A Research Paper." Belfast, Northern Ireland: Northern Ireland Community Relations Commission.

Davitt, M. 1904. *The Fall of Feudalism in Ireland*. London: Harper & Brothers.

De Baróid, C. 1990. *Ballymurphy and the Irish War*. London: Pluto.

——— 2000. *Ballymurphy and the Irish war*. New ed. London: Pluto.

Department of Health, Social Services, and Public Safety. 2005. "Strategic Resources Framework. HPSS Expenditure Plans for Northern Ireland by Programme of Care, Key Service and Locality, Incorporating Selected Planned Activity and Outcome Measures." Belfast, Ireland: Department of Health, Social Services, and Public Safety.

Devenport, M. 2000. *Flash Frames: Twelve Years Reporting Belfast*. Belfast, Ireland: Blackstaff.

Dillon, M. 1996. *25 Years of Terror*. Toronto, London: Bantam.

Dixit, A. K. 2004. *Lawlessness and Economics: Alternative Modes of Governance*. Princeton; Oxford: Princeton University Press.

Downes, D., and P. Rock. 1995. *Understanding Deviance. A Guide to the Sociology of Crime and Rule Breaking*. Rev. 2nd ed. Oxford: Clarendon.

Dunn, S., V. Morgan, and H. Dawson. 2000. *Attitudes to the Criminal Justice System. Northern Ireland Office Research Report Number 12*. Belfast, Northern Ireland: Northern Ireland Office Statistics and Research Branch.

Einwohner, R. L. 2003. "Opportunity, Honor and Action in the Warsaw Ghetto Uprising of 1943." *American Journal of Sociology* 109, no. 2 (September): 650–75.

Elster, J. 1999. *Alchemies of the Mind: Rationality and the Emotions*. Cambridge: Cambridge University Press.

Emler, N., and S. Reicher. 1995. *Adolescence and Delinquency*. Oxford: Blackwell.

Fagan, J. 1990. "Social Processes of Delinquency and Drug Use among Urban Gangs." In *Gangs in America*, edited by C. R. Huff. London: Sage Publications.

Farrington, D. 1983. "Randomized Experiments in Crime and Justice." Pp. 257–308 in *Crime and Justice*, edited by M. Tonry and N. Norris. Chicago: University of Chicago Press.

Farrington, D. P. 1997. "Human Development and Criminal Careers." In *The Oxford Handbook of Criminology*, edited by M. Maguire, R. Morgan, and R. Reiner. 2nd ed. Oxford: Clarendon.

Fay, M.-T., M. Morrissey, and M Smyth. 1999. *Northern Ireland's Troubles—The Human Costs*. London: Pluto.

Fay, M.-T., M. Morrissey, M. Smyth, and T. Wong. 1999. *The Costs of the Troubles Study. Report on the Northern Ireland Survey: The Experience and Impact of the Troubles*. Derry, Northern Ireland: INCORE.

Felman, Y. M., and F. J. Santora. 1981. "The Use of Condoms by VD Patients. A Survey." *Cutis* 27: 330–36.

Frank, R. H. 1985. *Choosing the Right Pond: Human Behaviour and the Quest for Status*. New York, Oxford: Oxford University Press.

———.1988. *Passions within Reason: The Strategic Role of the Emotions*. New York and London: Norton.

Friedman, M. 1962. *Capitalism and Freedom*. Chicago: University of Chicago Press.

Gambetta, D. 1993. *The Sicilian Mafia: The Business of Private Protection*. Cambridge, London: Harvard University Press.

———. 2009. *Crimes and Signs. Cracking the Codes of the Underworld*. Princeton: Princeton University Press.

Gambetta, D., and H. Hamill. 2005. *Streetwise: How Taxi Drivers Establish Customer's Trustworthiness*. New York: Russell Sage Foundation.

Geddis, P. W., R. Beatty, and M. Tyrrell. 1997. *Focus on Northern Ireland. A Statistical Profile. Northern Ireland Office Statistics and Research Agency*. London: The Stationery Office.

Gill, O. 1977. *Luke Street: Housing Policy, Conflict and the Creation of the Delinquent Area*. Basingstoke, England: Macmillan.

Gold, M. 1970. *Delinquent Behavior in an American City*. Belmont, Calif.: Brooks/Cole Publishing.

Gordon, D. 2002. "Loyalism at the crossroads: Part II, It's about fear." *Belfast Telegraph*, October 1.

Graham, J., and B. Bowling. 1995. *Young People and Crime. Home Office Research Study No. 145*. London: Home Office.

Greif, A. 2006. *Institutions and the Path to the Modern Economy: Lessons from Medieval Trade*. Cambridge, New York: Cambridge University Press.

Greif, A., P. Milgrom, and B. R. Weingast. 1994. "Coordination, Commitment and Enforcement: The Case of the Merchant Guild." *Journal of Political Economy* 102: 745–76.

Hagan, J. 1991. "Destiny and Drift: Subcultural Preferences, Status Attainments, and the Risks and Rewards of Youth". *American Sociological Review* 56, no. 5(October): 576–82.

Hagell, A., and T. Newburn. 1994. *Persistent Young Offenders*. London: Policy Studies Institute.

Hamill, H. 1999. *Against the Odds: The West Belfast Youth at Risk Programme*. Belfast, Northern Ireland: Probation Board for Northern Ireland.

Hammersley, M. 1992. *What's Wrong with Ethnography?* London, New York: Routledge.

Hammersley, M., and P. Atkinson. 1995. *Ethnography: Principles in Practice*. London; New York: Routledge.

Harkin, C., and A. Kilmurray. 1985. "Working with Women in Derry." Pp. 38–45 in *Women and Community Work in Northern Ireland*, edited by M. Abbott and H. Frazer. Belfast, Northern Ireland: Farset Co-operative Press.

Hayes, B., and I. McAllister. 2001. "Sowing Dragon's Teeth: Public Support for Political Violence and Paramilitarism in Northern Ireland." *Political Studies* 49, no. 6 (December): 901–22.

———. 2004. "Public Support for Political Violence and Paramilitarism." Pp. 50–66 in *Nothing but Trouble? Religion and the Irish Problem*, edited by D. Kennedy. Belfast, Northern Ireland: The Irish Association for Cultural, Economic and Social Relations.

———. 2005. "Public Support for Political Violence and Paramilitarism in Northern Ireland and the Republic of Ireland." *Terrorism and Political Violence* 17, no. 4: 599–617.

Her Majesty's Court Service. 2005. "Magistrates Courts Business Returns (BR Report) Annual Report 2004–2005." London: Department for Constitutional Affairs.

Herrnstein, R. 1995. "Criminogenic Traits." In *Crime*, edited by J. Q. Wilson and J. Petersilia. San Francisco, Calif.: Institute for Contemporary Studies Press.

Heskin, K. 1984. "The Psychology of Terrorism in Northern Ireland." In *Terrorism in Ireland*, edited by Y. Alexander and A. O'Day. London: Croom Helm.

Hill, P.B.E. 2003. *The Japanese Mafia: Yakuza, Law, and the State*. Oxford: Oxford University Press.

Hillyard, P. 1985. "Popular Justice in Northern Ireland: Communities and Change." Pp. 247–67 in *Research in Law, Deviance and Social Control*, vol. 7, edited by S. Spitzer and A. T. Scull. Greenwich, Conn., London: JAI Press.

Hillyard, P., G. Kelly, E. McLaughlin, D. Patsios, and M. Tomlinson. 2003. *Bare Necessities: Poverty and Social Exclusion in Northern Ireland*. Belfast, Northern Ireland: Democratic Dialogue.

Hillyard, P., and M. Tomlinson. 2000. "Patterns of Policing and Policing Patten." *Journal of Law and Society* 27, no. 3 (September): 394–415.

Hobbs, D. 1997. "Criminal Collaboration: Youth Gangs, Subcultures, Professional Criminals, and Organized Crime". In *The Oxford Handbook of Criminology*, edited by M. Morgan, R. Maguire, and R. Reiner. 2nd ed. Oxford: Clarendon.

Holland, J., and H. McDonald. 2001. "Mural to IRA 'peacemakers' is condemned." *The Observer* [London]. May 20.

Howe, L. 1990. *Being Unemployed in Northern Ireland: An Ethnographic Study.* Cambridge: Cambridge University Press.

Hughes, L. A., and J. F. Short. 2005. "Disputes Involving Youth Street Gang Members: Micro-social Contexts." *Criminology* 43, no. 1 (February): 43–76.

Human Rights Watch. 1991. *"Human Rights in Northern Ireland—A Helsinki Watch Report."* New York, London: Human Rights Watch.

———. 1997. *"To Serve Without Favour: Policing, Human Rights and Accountability in Northern Ireland."* New York, London: Human Rights Watch.

Humphreys, L. 1970. *Tearoom Trade: A Study of Homosexual Encounters in Public Places.* London: Duckworth.

Independent Monitoring Commission (IMC). 2004. "First Report of the Independent Monitoring Commission." London: The Stationery Office.

———. 2005a. "Fifth Report of the Independent Monitoring Commission." London: The Stationery Office.

———. 2005b. "Seventh Report of the Independent Monitoring Commission." London: The Stationery Office.

———. 2007a. "Thirteenth Report of the Independent Monitoring Commission." London: The Stationery Office.

———. 2007b. "Fifteenth Report of the Independent Monitoring Commission." London: The Stationery Office.

Jankowski, M. S. 1991. *Islands in the Street: Gangs and American Urban Society.* Berkeley; Oxford: University of California Press.

Jarman, N. 2004. "From War to Peace? Changing Patterns of Violence in Northern Ireland, 1990–2003." *Terrorism and Political Violence* 16, no. 3: 420–38.

Jarman, N., and D. Bryan. 1996. *Parade and Protest: A Discussion of Parading Disputes in Northern Ireland.* Coleraine, Northern Ireland: University of Ulster, Centre for the Study of Conflict.

Katz, J. 1988. *Seductions of Crime. Moral and Sensual Attractions in Doing Evil.* New York: Basic Books.

Kelley, K. J. 1982. *The Longest War: Northern Ireland and the IRA.* London: Zed.

Kennedy, L., ed. 1995. Crime and Punishment in West Belfast. Belfast, Northern Ireland: The Summer School. West Belfast.

———. August 2001. "They Shoot Children Don't They? An Analysis of the Age and Gender of Victims of Paramilitary 'Punishments' in Northern Ireland." A report prepared for the Northern Ireland Committee Against Terror (NICAT) and the Northern Ireland Affairs Committee of the House of Commons. Available at *http://cain.ulst.ac.uk/issues/violence/docs/kennedy01.htm*. Accessed March 24, 2010.

Klein, M. W. 1995. *The American Street Gang: Its Nature, Prevalence and Control.* New York, Oxford: Oxford University Press.

Knox, C. 2002. "See No Evil, Hear No Evil': Insidious Paramilitary Violence in Northern Ireland." *The British Journal of Criminology* 42, no. 1 (winter): 164–85.

Lee, R. M. 1993. *Doing Research on Sensitive Topics.* London: Sage Publications.

Leonard, M. 1994. *Informal Economic Activity in Belfast.* Aldershot, Englandd: Avebury.

———. 2004. "Bonding and Bridging Social Capital: Reflections from Belfast." *Sociology* 38, no. 5: 927–44.

Lerman, P. 1967. "Gangs, Networks, and Subcultural Delinquency." *American Journal of Sociology* 73, no. 1: 63–72.

Levi, M. 1997. "Violent Crime." In *The Oxford Handbook of Criminology,* edited by M. Maguire, R. Morgan and R. Reiner. 2nd ed. Oxford: Clarendon.

Lewis, H. 1989. *Insuring against Burglary Losses.* London: Home Office.

Lister, D., and H. Jordan. 2003. *Mad Dog: The Rise and Fall of Johnny Adair and 'C' Company.* Edinburgh: Mainstream.

Little, M., J. Kogan, R. Bullock, and P. Van Der Laan. 2004. "ISSP: An Experiment in Multi-Systemic Responses to Persistent Young Offenders Known to Children's Services." *British Journal of Criminology* 44, no. 2 (March): 225–40.

Lofland, J. 1969. *Deviance and Identity.* Upper Saddle River, N.J.: Prentice-Hall, Inc.

MacStiofáin, S. 1975. *Revolutionary in Ireland.* London: G. Cremonesi.

Maguire, M. 1982. *Burglary in a Dwelling: The Offence, the Offender, and the Victim.* London: Heinemann.

———. 1997. "Crime Statistics, Patterns and Trends: Changing Perceptions and Their Implications." Pp. 135–88 in *The Oxford Handbook of Criminology,* edited by M. Maguire, R. Morgan, and R. Reiner. 2nd ed. Oxford: Clarendon.

Matza, D. 1964. *Delinquency and Drift: From the Research Program of the Center for the Study of Law and Society, University of California, Berkeley.* New York: Wiley.

Maxson, C. L., and M. W. Klein. 1990. "Street Gang Violence: Twice as Great or Half as Great?" Pp. 71–102 in *Gangs in America,* edited by C. R. Huff. Newbury Park, Calif.: Sage Publications.

Mays, J. B. 1954. *Growing Up in the City: A Study of Juvenile Delinquency in an Urban Neighbourhood.* Liverpool, England: Liverpool University Press.

McAleer, K. 1994. *Dueling: The Cult of Honor in Fin-de-siècle Germany.* Princeton: Princeton University Press.

McCaffrey, B. 2003a. "Shootings linked to failed UDA coup bid." *Irish News* [Belfast], October 23.

———. 2003b. "Rights activist scorns UDA humiliation move." *Irish News* [Belfast], March 20.

———. 2004. "A Historic Turning Point but the Road Ahead Was Hard; 10 Years after the Ceasefires." *Irish News* [Belfast], July 26.

McCracken, G. 1988. *The Long Interview.* London: Sage Publications.

McCullough, D., T. Schmidt, and B. Lockart. 1990. *Car Theft in Northern Ireland: Recent Studies on a Persistent Problem.* Belfast, Northern Ireland: Extern.

McDonald, H. 1996. "UVF 'fines' former leader £30,000." *Sunday Times* [London], December 15.

McDonald, H., and J. Cusack. 2004. *UDA: Inside the Heart of Loyalist Terror.* London: Penguin.

McDonald, Z. 2001. "Revisiting the Dark Figure: A Microeconometric Analysis of the Under-reporting of Property Crime and Its Implications." *British Journal of Criminology* 41, no. 1 (winter): 127–49.

McElrath, K. 2004. "Drug use and drug markets in the context of political conflict: The case of Northern Ireland." *Addiction Research and Theory* 12, no. 6 (December): 577–90.

McEvoy, K. 2000. "Law, Struggle, and Political Transformation in Northern Ireland." *Journal of Law and Society* 27, no. 3 (September): 542–71.

McGarry, J., and B. O'Leary. 1999. *Policing Northern Ireland: Proposals for a New Start.* Belfast, Northern Ireland: Blackstaff.

McGuffin, J. 1973. *Internment.* Tralee, Ireland: Anvil Books.

McGuinness, M. 1999. "Belfast conference as Upper Springfield goes live." *An Phoblacht/Republican News* [Belfast] March 3.

McKittrick, D. 1999. "Four attacked in N. Ireland 'punishment shootings.'" *The Independent* [London], January 7.

———. 2005. "How has the IRA changed? Once it shot you in the knees, now it's in the hands." *The Independent* [London], February 6.

———. 2007. "David Ervine; Progressive Unionist Party leader." *The Independent* [London], January 9.

McQuoid, J. 1994. "The Self-Reported Delinquency Study in Belfast, Northern Ireland." In *Delinquent Behavior among Young People in the Western World. First Results of the International Self-Report Delinquency Study*, edited by J. Junger-Tas, G.-T. Terlaun, and M. W. Klein. Amsterdam: Kugler.

McWilliams, M. 1995. "Masculinity and Violence: A Gender Perspective on Policing and Crime in Northern Ireland." In *Crime and Punishment in West Belfast*, edited by L Kennedy. Belfast, Northern Ireland: The Summer School. West Belfast.

Melaugh, M. 1994. *Majority Minority Review 3: Housing and Religion in Northern Ireland.* Coleraine, Ireland: Centre for the Study of Conflict, University of Ulster.

Miles, M. B., and A. M. Huberman. 1994. *Qualitative Data Analysis: An Expanded Sourcebook.* 2nd ed. London: Sage.

Miller, W. 1958. "Lower Class Culture as a Generating Milieu of Gang Delinquency." *Journal of Social Issues* 14, no. 3: 5–19.

Miller, W. 1990. *Bloodtaking and Peacemaking: Feud, Law and Society in Saga.* Chicago, London: University of Chicago Press.

Moloney, E. 2002. *A Secret History of the IRA.* London: Allen Lane.

Monaghan, R. 2004. "'An Imperfect Peace': Paramilitary Punishments in Northern Ireland." *Terrorism and Political Violence* 16, no. 3: 439–61.

Moriarty, G. 1998. "First batch of released prisoners beginning of process." *The Irish Times.* [Dublin]. September 12.

Morrison, S., and O'Donnell, I. 1994. *Armed Robbery: A Study in London.* Occasional Paper, No. 15. Oxford: University of Oxford, Centre for Criminological Research.

Morrissey, M. 1980. "The Limits of Community Action." M. Phil. diss., Ulster Polytechnic, Jordanstown.

Morrissey, M., and K. Pease. 1982. "The Black Criminal Justice System in West Belfast." *The Howard Journal* 21 (July): 159–66.

Munck, R. 1988. "The Lads and the Hoods: Alternative Justice in and Irish Context." In *Whose Law and Order? Aspects of Crime and Social Control in Irish Society*, edited by M. Thomlinson, T. Varley, and C. McCullough. Belfast, Northern Ireland: Sociological Association of Ireland.

Murphy, C. 2001. "Doctors face task of treating nightmare injuries. Medical practitioners tell Clare Murphy of the devastating physical and psychological effects 'punishment attacks' have on their victims." *The Irish Times* [Dublin], May 23.

Murray, G. 2002. "We shot Mahood for treason says UDA; He committed a crime and had to be dealt with." *Belfast News Letter,* November 2.

———. 2003. "Name and Shame Challenge to Republicans." *Belfast News Letter,* March 22.

Nagin, D.S. 1998. "Criminal Deterrence Research at the Outset of the Twenty-First Century." *Crime and Justice: A Review of Research* 23: 1–42.

Neill, G. 2005. "Naming viewed as 'way forward' but inadequate." *Irish News* [Belfast], March 5.

Nelson, S. 1984. *Ulster's Uncertain Defenders: Protestant Political, Paramilitary and Community Groups and the Northern Ireland Conflict.* Belfast, Northern Ireland: Appletree.

Nicholas, R. M., R. J. Barr, and R.A.B. Mollan. 1993. "Paramilitary Punishment in Northern Ireland: A Macabre Irony." *Journal of Trauma* 34: 90–95.

Noble, M., H. Barnes, G. Smith, D. McLennan, C. Dibben, D. Avenell, T. Smith, C. Anttila, M. Sigala, and C. Mokhtar. 2005. *Northern Ireland Multiple Deprivation Measures, 2005.* Belfast, Northern Ireland: Northern Ireland Statistics and Research Agency.

North Belfast Advice Consortium. 1999. *Addressing Local Needs.* Belfast, Northern Ireland: Community Development Centre, North Belfast.

Northern Ireland Affairs Committee. 2001. *Select Committee on Northern Ireland Affairs Third Report. Relocation Following Paramilitary Intimidation.* Vols. 1 and 2. March 28. London: House of Commons.

Northern Ireland Affairs Committee on Community Restorative Justice. 2006. *Minutes of Evidence taken before Northern Ireland Affairs Committee on Community Restorative Justice.* December 4. London: House of Commons.

Northern Ireland Neighbourhood Information Service. 2010. "Parliamentary Constituency Information for Belfast West." Belfast, Northern Ireland: Northern Ireland Statistics and Research Agency. Available at http://www.ninis.nisra.gov.uk/mapxtreme/report.asp?DESC=FromGeneral&CurrentLevel=AA&ID=4&Name=Belfast%20West. Accessed on March 14, 2010.

Northern Ireland Office, Statistics and Research Branch. 1997. *A Review of Statistical and Research Information on "Joyriding."* Belfast, Northern Ireland: Northern Ireland Office.

Northern Ireland Statistics and Research Agency. 2003. *Northern Ireland Census 2001 Standard Tables, Northern Ireland Assembly Papers, Session 2002/2003, 102/02.* London: The Stationery Office.

———. 2005. *Northern Ireland Multiple Deprivation Measure 2005*. May 2005. Belfast, Northern Ireland: Northern Ireland Statistics and Research Agency.

Oakley, A. 1981. "Interviewing Women: A Contradiction in Terms." In *Doing Feminist Research*, edited by H. Roberts. London: Routledge and Kegan Paul.

Oglaigh na hEireann. 2005. "Full text of IRA statement." *The Guardian* [London], March 8.

O'Connell, S. 2006. "From Toad of Toad Hall to the 'Death Drivers' of Belfast: An Exploratory History of 'Joyriding.'" *British Journal of Criminology* 46 no. 3 May: 455–69.

O'Connor, F. 1993. *In Search of a State: Catholics in Northern Ireland*. Belfast, Northern Ireland: Blackstaff.

O'Doherty, M. 1998. *The Trouble with Guns: Republican Strategy and the Provisional IRA*. Belfast, Northern Ireland: Blackstaff.

O'Neill, S. 2003. "Shocking Statistics of Loyalist Pipe Bombs." *Irish News* [Belfast], February 21.

Opinion. 1996. "Inhumanity of Gang Beatings." *Irish News* [Belfast].

Ousey, G. C. and M. R. Lee. 2004. "Investigating the Connections Between Race, Illicit Drug Markets, and Lethal Violence, 1984–1997." *Journal of Research in Crime and Delinquency* 41, no. 4 (November): 352–83.

Parker, H. J. 1974. *View From the Boys: A Sociology of Down Town Adolescents*. London, Vancouver: David and Charles.

Patrick, J. 1973. *A Glasgow Gang Observed*. London: Methuen.

Petersen, R. 2001. *Resistance and Rebellion: Lessons from Eastern Europe*. Cambridge: Cambridge University Press.

Picard, R. G. 1991. "How Violence Is Justified: Sinn Féin's An Phoblacht." *Journal of Communication* 41, no. 4 (December): 90–103.

Poland, T. 2000. "*A Report on the Logistics of Crime and Young People in West Belfast*." Belfast, Northern Ireland: Unpublished report commissioned by PBNI and presented at a meeting of the West Belfast Partnership Board, January.

Police Service of Northern Ireland (PSNI). 2003. "Casualties as a Result of Paramilitary-Style Attacks, 1973–2003, (By Calendar Year)." Belfast, Northern Ireland.

———. 2006a. "Statistical Report No 1. Recorded Crime and Clearances. 1st April 2005–31st March 2006." Belfast, Northern Ireland: A National Statistics Publication.

———2006b. "Chief Constable's Report 2005–2006." Belfast: Police Service for Northern Ireland.

———. 2009. "Casualties as a Result of Paramilitary-Style Attacks, 1973–2003, (By Calendar Year)," available at http://cain.ulst.ac.uk/ni/security.htm#11. Accessed March 24, 2010.

Police Service of Northern Ireland, Statistics and Research Unit. 2004. Reconviction data, edited by Heather Hamill. Belfast, Northern Ireland.

Posner, E. A. 2000. *Law and Social Norms*. Cambridge, Mass., London: Harvard University Press.

Radzinowicz, L., and J. King. 1977. *The Growth of Crime: The International Experience*. London: Hamish Hamilton.

Rea, E. 1994. "The Anatomy of Joyriding: A Study of Joyriding in West Belfast." Unpublished MSc. thesis. University of Ulster.

Robins, D., and P. Cohen. 1978. *Knuckle Sandwich: Growing Up in the Working-Class City*. Harmondsworth, England: Penguin.

Rock, P. 1997. "Sociological Theories of Crime." In *The Oxford Handbook of Criminology*, edited by M. Maguire, R. Morgan, and R. Reiner. 2nd ed. Oxford: Clarendon.

Rutter, M., H. Giller, and A. Hagell. 1998. *Anti-social Behaviour by Young People*. Cambridge: Cambridge University Press.

Scarman, The Hon. Mr. Justice. 1972. *Government of Northern Ireland Violence and Civil Disturbances in Northern Ireland in 1969: Report of Tribunal of Inquiry*. Belfast, Ireland: Her Majesty's Stationery Office.

Schneider, E. C. 1999. *Vampires, Dragons, and Egyptian Kings: Youth Gangs in Postwar New York*. Princeton: Princeton University Press.

Sherman, L. W., J. D. Schmidt, and D. P. Rogan. 1992. *Policing Domestic Violence: Experiments and Dilemmas*. New York: Free Press.

Shover, N., and D. Honaker. 1992. "The Socially Bounded Decision Making of Persistent Property Offenders." *The Howard Journal* 31, no. 4 (November): 276–93.

Silke, A. 1999. "Ragged Justice: Loyalist Vigilantism in Northern Ireland." *Terrorism and Political Violence* 11, no. 3 (autumn): 1–31.

Silke, A. 2000. "Drink, Drugs, Drugs, and Rock'n'Roll: Financing Loyalist Terrorism in Northern Ireland—Part Two." *Studies in Conflict and Terrorism* 23, no. 2 (January): 107–27.

Silke, A., and M. Taylor. 2000. "War Without End: IRA and Loyalist Vigilantism in Northern Ireland." *Howard Journal of Criminal Justice* 39, no. 3 (August): 249–66.

Silverman, D. 1993. *Qualitative Data: Methods for Analysing Talk, Text and Interaction*. London: Sage Publications.

Skogan, W. G. 1994. *Contacts Between Police and Public: Findings from the 1992 British Crime Survey*. London: Her Majesty's Stationery Office.

Sluka, J. A. 1989. *Hearts and Minds, Water and Fish: Support for the IRA and INLA in a Northern Irish Ghetto*. Greenwich, Conn., London: JAI Press.

Smyth, J. 1992. *The Men of No Property, Irish Radicals and Popular Politics in the Late Eighteenth Century*. Basingstoke, England: Macmillan.

South, N. 2002. "Drugs, Alcohol and Crime." Pp. 914–46 in *The Oxford Handbook of Criminology*, edited by M. Maguire, R. Morgan and R. Reiner. 3rd ed. Oxford: Oxford University Press.

Spence, M. 1973. "Job Market Signaling." Quarterly Journal of Economics 87, no. 3 (August): 355–74.

Spergel, I. A. 1992. "Youth Gangs: An Essay Review." *Social Service Review* 66: 121–40.

Stewart, A.T.Q. 1997. *The Narrow Ground: Aspects of Ulster, 1609–1969*. Belfast, Northern Ireland: Blackstaff.

Stevens, Sir J. 2003. "Stevens Enquiry Overview and Recommendations." Sir John Stevens QPM, DL. Commissioner of the Metropolitan Police Service. April 17.

Available at *http://cain.ulst.ac.uk/issues/collusion/stevens3/stevens3summary.htm*. Accessed March 24, 2010.

Sunday Times Insight Team. 1972. *Ulster*. London: André Deutsch.

Sutton, M. 1994. *Bear in mind these dead . . . An index of deaths from the conflict in Ireland, 1969–1993*. Belfast, Northern Ireland: Beyond the Pale.

———. 2002. "An Index of Deaths from the Conflict in Ireland." Belfast. Available at *http://cain.ulst.ac.uk/sutton/book/index.html*. Accessed March 12, 2010.

———. 2010 "An Index of Deaths from the Conflict in Ireland." Updated and revised. Available at *http://cain.ulst.ac.uk/sutton/*. Accessed March 24, 2010.

Taylor, P. 2000. *Loyalists*. London: Bloomsbury.

Tentler, T. N. 1977. *Sin and Confession on the Eve of the Reformation*. Princeton: Princeton University Press.

The Independent Commission on Policing for Northern Ireland. 1999. "A New Beginning: Policing in Northern Ireland. The Report of The Independent Commission on Policing for Northern Ireland." London: Her Majesty's Stationery Office.

Thompson, W., and B. Mulholland. 1995. "Paramilitary Punishments and Young People in West Belfast: Psychological Effects and the Implications for Education." In *Crime and Punishment in West Belfast*, edited by L Kennedy. Belfast, Northern Ireland: West Belfast Summer School.

Townshend, C. 1999. *Ireland: The 20th Century*. London: Arnold.

Tvetkova, M. 2008. "Wrestling for Supremacy: The Evolution of Extra-Legal Protection in Bulgaria." Unpublished D.Phil. diss., Department of Sociology, University of Oxford.

Varese, F. 1996. "The Emergence of the Russian Mafia: Dispute Settlement and Protection in a New Market Economy." D.Phil. diss., Department of Sociology, University of Oxford.

———. 2001. *The Russian Mafia: Private Protection in a New Market Economy*. Oxford: Oxford University Press.

———. 2006. "How Mafias Migrate: The Case of the`Ndrangheta in Northern Italy." *Law and Society Review* 40, no. 2 (June): 411–44.

Veblen, T. [1899] 1970. *The Theory of the Leisure Class: An Economic Study of Institutions*. 2nd ed. London: Allen and Unwin.

Venkatesh, S.A. 1997. "The Social Organization of Street Gang Activity in an Urban Ghetto." *American Journal of Sociology* 103, no. 1 (July): 82–111.

———. 2000. *American Project. The Rise and Fall of a Modern Ghetto*. Cambridge, Mass.;London: Harvard University Press.

Venkatesh, S. A., and S. D. Levitt. 2000. "Are we a family or a business?" History and Disjuncture in the Urban American Street Gang." *Theory and Society* 29, no. 4 (August): 427–62.

Von Hirsch, A. 1999. *Criminal Deterrence and Sentence Severity: An Analysis of Recent Research*. Oxford: Hart.

Walsh, D. 1980. *Break-Ins. Burglary from Private Houses*. London: Constable.

Watt, N. 2000. "Paratrooper Lee Clegg Cleared of Last Charge over Death of Teenagers." *The Guardian* [London], February 1.

Wax, M. L., and J. Cassell. 1979. "Fieldwork Ethics and Politics: The Wider Context." Pp. 85–102 in *Federal Regulation: Ethical Issues and Social Research*. Boulder, Colo.: Westview Press.

Weitzer, R. J. 1995. *Policing under Fire: Ethnic Conflict and Police-Community Relations in Northern Ireland*. Albany: State University of New York Press.

West Belfast Economic Forum. 2005. "A Bibliography of West Belfast." Belfast, Northern Ireland: West Belfast Economic Forum. Available at *http://www.wbef.org/bibliography.htm*. Accessed February 1, 2005.

Whyte, W. F. 1981. *Street Corner Society: The Social Structure of an Italian Slum*. 3rd ed., revised and expanded. Chicago, London: University of Chicago Press.

Wilson, McLiam, R. 1996. *Eureka Street*. London: Secker & Warburg.

———. 1997. *Ripley Bogle*. London: Minerva.

Winston, T. 1997. "Alternatives to Punishment Beatings and Shootings in a Loyalist Community in Belfast." *Critical Criminology* 8, no. 1 (March): 122–28.

Wolfgang, M. E., M. F. Robert, and S. Thorstein. 1972. *Delinquency in a Birth Cohort*. Chicago: University of Chicago Press.

Wood, E. J. 2003. *Insurgent Collective Action and Civil War in El Salvador*. Cambridge: Cambridge University Press.

Wright, R. T., and S. H. Decker. 1994. *Burglars on the Job: Streetlife and Residential Break-ins*. Boston: Northeastern University Press.

Yin, R. K. 1994. *Case Study Research: Design and Methods*. 2nd ed. Thousand Oaks, Calif., London: Sage Publications.

Zahavi, A., and A. Zahavi. 1997. *The Handicap Principle: A Missing Piece in Darwin's Puzzle*. Oxford: Oxford University Press.

Zedner, L. 1994. "Victims." Pp. 1207–46 in *The Oxford Handbook of Criminology*, edited by M. Maguire, R. Morgan, and R. Reiner. 2nd ed. Oxford: Clarendon.

———. 1997. "Victims." Pp. 577– 612 in *The Oxford Handbook of Criminology*, edited by M. Maguire, R. Morgan, and R. Reiner. 2nd ed. Oxford: Clarendon.

INDEX